TIME IN YOUR LIFE

When was it noon twice on the same day in many parts of the United States?

Where can you make an appointment for yesterday and keep it?

How can you tell time by a crab?

What animal hibernates daily, not just winters?

Who is responsible for February's having only 28 days?

Why is your watch regulator called a "hair" spring?

These questions suggest a few of the fascinating pieces of information to be found in *Time in Your Life*. There have been one or two books about clocks and calendars, but we believe that no author previously has taken the entire subject of *time* for a book for young people. So broad is the subject that it takes us into many fields of knowledge, discussing the stars and planets (man's oldest time-pieces); rocks and rivers; history and the calendar; clocks and watches; time zones; rhythms of organic life; rhythms of the universe and of the atom; music and dancing, etc., etc.

Books by Irving Adler

COLOR IN YOUR LIFE
DUST
THE ELEMENTARY MATHEMATICS OF THE ATOM
FIRE IN YOUR LIFE
HOT AND COLD
HOW LIFE BEGAN
INSIDE THE NUCLEUS
LOGIC FOR BEGINNERS
MAGIC HOUSE OF NUMBERS
MAN-MADE MOONS
MONKEY BUSINESS: *Hoaxes in the Name of Science*
A NEW LOOK AT ARITHMETIC
THE NEW MATHEMATICS
PROBABILITY AND STATISTICS FOR EVERY MAN
THE SECRET OF LIGHT
SEEING THE EARTH FROM SPACE
THE STARS: *Stepping Stones into Space*
THE SUN AND ITS FAMILY
THINKING MACHINES
TIME IN YOUR LIFE
TOOLS IN YOUR LIFE
THE TOOLS OF SCIENCE
WEATHER IN YOUR LIFE
WHAT WE WANT OF OUR SCHOOLS

IRVING ADLER

Time in Your Life

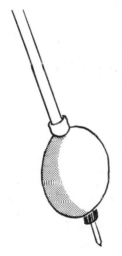

Illustrated by Ruth Adler

The John Day Company
New York

THANKS are due to the Hamilton Watch Company for permission
to reproduce the drawing of a balance wheel from their booklet
on "Time Telling." The author also expresses his appreciation to
Sentinel Books for permission to use in this book the directions
for making a sundial which he wrote for *Discover the Stars.*

Library of Congress Catalog Card Number: 68-8611

MANUFACTURED IN THE UNITED STATES OF AMERICA
BY THE MURRAY PRINTING COMPANY, FORGE VILLAGE, MASS.

Contents

CHAPTER I

Living in Time

The Time Of Your Life: The Present

YOU live in an *ocean* of space, but you live in a *river* of time. Space surrounds you on all sides, but time flows past you in a steady stream.

Your place in time is *the present*, or *now*. But *now* is a very slippery thing. You can't hold on to it at all. It won't even stay with you as long as it takes to say the word. Because just as fast as something happens it becomes part of the past, and, forever after, you may talk about it only as something that *has* happened.

Every moment is a new *now*. Your life is made up of a stream of *nows* arranged like beads on a string, and slipping past you in a steady flow. The future becomes the present, the present becomes the past, and the past moves on behind you never to return.

There are times when you have done something wrong and you say, "I wish I had it to do over. I wouldn't make *that* mistake again!" But you know you can't do it over, because once it's done it's gone. But while you can't do a thing *over*, sometimes you can do it *again*. In such cases, although you can't wipe out the mistakes of the past, at least you can learn from those mistakes and try not to repeat them.

Time Marches On

There are occasions when you have a lot of things to do, and you just know you won't have enough time to finish. You rush and you rush, racing against time. Sometimes you wish time would stand still, but you know it's no use, because time won't stop for anybody.

The men and women who make the laws for New York State face that problem in Albany every year. The legislature always chooses in advance the day on which it will close its session or adjourn. Every year, when that day arrives, there is a frantic rush to finish the business of the session before the day is over. Bills are killed at great speed, or passed and sent to the Governor for his signature. And every year, as midnight of the last day approaches, they find that they still have more work to do and time is running out. They dare not work on past midnight, because action they take after the official closing time will not count. But they must work on to be able to finish at all. What should they do? The legislators solve this problem each year by *stopping the clock* before midnight. Then, while they work on into the small hours of the next morning, their clock shows that all the action they take happens before the official closing time. This is the game of make-believe they are forced to play because, although they have the power to make our laws, they do not have the power to make time stand still.

When they stop the clock, the New York lawmakers are acting out a modern imitation of the story of Joshua. Joshua is the biblical military leader who commanded the children of Israel after the death of Moses. When he led his soldiers in battle against the Amorites, he was worried that night might fall before he was sure of victory. He solved that

problem by ordering the Sun and Moon to stand still. "And," the Bible tells us, "the Sun stood still, and the Moon stayed, until the people had avenged themselves upon their enemies."

Ponce de León wanted to stop the flow of time for another reason. He didn't like the idea of growing old, so he went searching for the Fountain of Youth. He hoped that by drinking its magic water he would be able to prolong his life. He set out to look for it in 1513, and discovered Florida instead. Today we don't believe in any Fountain of Youth, but we have been more successful than de León was in prolonging life. By conquering disease and improving the conditions of life we have added many years to the average life span. The average length of life in de Léon's time was about 35 years. Today in the United States it is about 70 years.

Time Is A One-Way Street

Once I saw a very strange sight on a motion picture screen. A girl had just jumped off a diving board into a swimming pool. Then she jumped up out of the water, rising from the surface feet first, and landed on her feet on the diving board! You have probably guessed what happened. The operator of the motion picture projector stopped the machine after the dive, and then ran the film backwards. In this way you can make things happen backwards on the screen. You can do the same thing with a sound track. Run a sound tape record of a song backwards, and it will sound like Donald Duck having a nightmare! But, while you can run a movie or a sound track backwards, you can't do the same thing with time. The flow of time is always in one direction only, from the past, through the present, and on into the future.

The Secrets Of The Past

People are fascinated by mysteries. They like to solve puzzles. There is adventure in exploring unknown regions. Because we can't reverse the flow of time, the past is an unknown region, challenging us to conquer its secrets. That is why so many science fiction stories are written about time machines that are supposed to carry you back into the past or forward into the future.

Time machines are fun to read about, but they aren't real. But there are ways in which we really can explore the past. For a part of the past, we can find out what happened long ago from written records that people have left behind. From newspapers or from books, from letters people wrote to each other, or even from inscriptions carved on

12

monuments, we can piece together the story of what happened. Putting all the scraps of information together is like solving a jigsaw puzzle, and often some of the parts are missing. But the more difficult the puzzle is, the more exciting it is to solve it.

Cracking The Code

A few hundred years ago people who studied the written records already knew many things about life in ancient Rome 2,000 years ago. They had no trouble understanding these records because they were written in Latin, a language they understood. But they weren't so successful in studying the life of ancient Egypt. The inscriptions of the ancient Egyptians were written in a picture language called hieroglyphics. This language had died out long before this time, and no one knew what the picture symbols meant. Trying to read the inscriptions was like trying to read a message in code without having the key to the code. But all this was changed by a very lucky find. In the year 1799, men digging among the ruins near Rosetta, Egypt, found a stone that had the same inscription in three written languages. One was the ancient hieroglyphics; the second was a later form of Egyptian writing; and the third was the Greek language, which was very well understood. This provided the key for cracking the code and exploring more of the secrets of the past of ancient Egypt.

Stories Told Without Words

Today scientists are exploring the secrets of another ancient kingdom, located in western India. They call it the

13

Harappa civilization because the village of Harappa now stands where this kingdom flourished over 4,000 years ago. Although they have found written records there, they can't read them, because nobody understands the language. Unless a "Rosetta Stone" is found for this language, the messages in these written records may remain a secret forever.

But there are other messages this ancient people left which the scientists can read. These are messages without words, dug up out of the ruins. Just as a good detective can reconstruct the story of a crime from a footprint, a piece of hair, a pinch of dust, or a stain, an archeologist can reconstruct the story of what happened thousands of years ago from the clues that he finds. The remains of ancient buildings, the tools the people used, the contents of their graves, and even their rubbish heaps, are all clues that help us to understand how the people lived and worked, and even how they were ruled.

Stories In The Rocks

Written records and old ruins take us back only a few thousand years into the past. But there are other clues that help us understand what happened hundreds of millions of years ago. These clues are the rocks we find in the ground. Every rock tells a story, and the geologist knows how to read this story. For example, coal tells a story about giant ferns in a buried swamp. Limestone tells a story about ancient seas that have disappeared. Fossils tell about the life of the past and how it has changed. These are some of the clues that have helped us pierce the darkness of the dead past as far back as two billion years ago.

14

Seeing The Past With Your Own Eyes

In history, archeology, and geology we figure out what the past was like by piecing together the clues we find. But there is one place where we can actually *see* the past with our own eyes. Look up at a star in the sky. The light from that star reaches us only after a long journey in space. For example, although Sirius, the brightest star we can see in the winter sky, is one of the stars that is nearest to us, it takes nine years for its light to reach us. That means that when we look at Sirius we see, not what it looks like now, but what it looked like nine years ago. The great nebula in Andromeda, a faint patch of light barely visible to the naked eye, is so far away that it takes two million years for its light to reach us. So when we look at this nebula we are looking two million years back into the past.

The Mystery Of The Future

The past has its secrets that are buried or forgotten. The future has the mystery of the unborn and unknown. Although the flow of time carries us forward steadily into the future, it does so at its own unhurried rate. And as tomorrow becomes today, there are always new tomorrows, and the mystery of the future remains.

In your neighborhood movie house you see previews of coming attractions. Is it possible to see previews of the future? For thousands of years people have hoped that they could, and they have tried in many ways to pierce the veil of mystery that hides the future from their eyes.

There are fortunetellers who claim that they can forecast the future by looking into a crystal ball, by reading your palm or tea leaves, or by looking at the positions of the

15

planets in the sky. These are just fakers, and the only thing they can predict with certainty is that their customers will have less money after seeing them than before.

But there are real prophets who *can* foretell the future, sometimes with amazing accuracy. These are the scientists in various fields of study where the laws of nature are understood quite well. With their knowledge of the past and present, their understanding of the laws of nature helps them predict what to expect in the future. The meteorologist, for example, forecasts the weather. Sometimes he makes mistakes, because our knowledge of the laws of weather is still incomplete. But the astronomer knows so well how the earth and moon move that he can predict an eclipse of the sun years in advance, and be accurate to a fraction of a second.

Our knowledge of the laws of nature gives us more than the power of prediction. It gives us the power to control and direct the forces of nature, and the power to direct ourselves. This makes it possible for us to make plans and go to work to carry them out. The more we understand

about nature, the more we can influence the way things happen. As we make progress in the study and use of science it will be more and more correct to say that *the future will be what we make it.*

Keeping Track Of Time

Your birth certificate tells when you were born. Since that day your parents (and later, you) have reckoned how much time has passed, so that they would know how old you are. They did this because they liked to watch you grow, but also because they had to keep track of your age. When you were a baby, your doctor needed this information before he could decide when to start you on new foods and when to give you inoculations against disease. Your school needs this information now to know which grade to put you in. To have this information it is necessary to have a system of keeping track of time, or measuring it.

The measurement of time is important in all things people do. It is important in work. This is shown in the saying "Time is money." In a factory, time wasted is money lost. The measurement of time is also important in recreation. You look at the calendar to know when your next vacation will begin. You look at the clock to know when to tune in your favorite TV program. And you can be sure the stage manager of that show had everything timed to the second, to make a smoothly running program that begins and ends on time.

Measuring time is so much a part of our daily lives that we hardly give it any thought. We look at a watch to see what time it is, without asking what makes the watch so clever that it can tell us what we ourselves don't know. And, for most of us, a calendar is merely a souvenir we get from

17

a neighborhood store during Christmas week. But built into each of these are hundreds of years of practical experience and scientific study. And hidden in each, too, are interesting facts, exciting stories, and fascinating puzzles. You can get a preview of them now by looking at the table of contents of this book.

Feeling The Pulse Of Nature

To measure a distance we use a ruler. The lines on the ruler divide the distance into equal pieces which we can count. The number of pieces is the measure of the distance. You measure the length of your room by counting the number of feet in it. You measure the width of this book by counting the number of inches in it. To measure time we have to be able to divide time into equal pieces that we can count. But we can't print lines on time the way we do on a ruler. Then how do we mark off the equal pieces of time? We do it by using something that happens over and over again, beating out a regular rhythm.

Thousands of years ago, when men first became aware of the need to measure time, they noticed at the same time many rhythms in nature. They found rhythms in the sky, and rhythms on the ground. They found rhythms in life, and rhythms in lifeless things. And the more they learned about nature, the more rhythms they found. By using these rhythms, by feeling the pulse of nature, they worked out many ways of measuring time. Each new rhythm they discovered gave them another way of measuring time. That is why this story of time is the story of the rhythm of the universe.

CHAPTER II

The Clock We Never Wind

THERE are wrist watches that are advertised as self-winding. You don't have to wind such a watch by turning a winding stem because it is wound by the movements of the arm on which you wear it. But there is another clock which you never have to wind at all. It is with you all the time, although you never carry it. It moves steadily and keeps accurate time. In fact, it is so accurate that we set all our other clocks by it. This clock that we never wind is the *earth*. The rhythm of the earth that keeps time for us is the rhythm with which it spins on its axis.

The Rhythm Of The Earth—Star Time

When you ride on a merry-go-round, as it turns around it looks as though the merry-go-round is standing still while

19

all the things surrounding it are turning in the opposite direction. The rhythm with which the merry-go-round turns is shown by the rhythm with which the surroundings seem to turn.

The earth is like a big merry-go-round. It spins like a top. Because the spinning is so steady, we don't feel it. But we do notice the spinning in the fact that all the things surrounding the earth look as though they are turning around it in the opposite direction. People discovered this fact thousands of years ago by looking at the sky. If we watch the sky ourselves night after night we can see it too. The sky looks like a big bowl that is upside down, with us inside it. The stars look like little spots of light on the inside of the bowl. They look as though they are pasted on, because they have a definite arrangement, and they keep their places all the time. This is because they are so far away that their movements cannot be noticed with the naked eye. We have learned to recognize groups of stars that are in the same part of the sky. We call them constellations. If we watch these constellations during the night we will see that the sky seems to be turning all the time.

If you face north and look at the sky on a clear night, one constellation that you can recognize very easily is the Big Dipper. The diagram shows you what it looks like. The two stars in the dipper that are farthest from the handle are called the pointers, because a line drawn through them points to Polaris, the North Star. Polaris is the end of the handle of the Little Dipper, which looks as though it is pouring into the Big Dipper. On the other side of Polaris, away from the Big Dipper, is a constellation that looks like a big "W." It is called Cassiopeia.

If you watch these constellations for a few hours at night you will see that, while the stars all keep their places, the whole sky is turning. The center around which it turns is called the *pole*. It is near Polaris, so Polaris doesn't seem to move much. But the Big Dipper and Cassiopeia turn around the pole like the hands of a big clock. In fact, in Chapter IV I shall explain how you can use them as the hands of a clock to tell time by the stars. The diagram on this page shows you what the northern sky looks like at

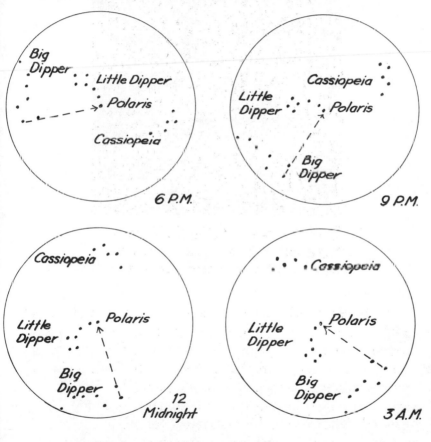

Northern Sky at 3 Hour Intervals
on September 21

different times on September 21st. Notice that the direction in which the sky turns is counterclockwise, that is, the opposite of the direction in which the hands of a clock move.

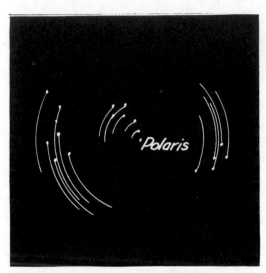

Star tracks of the Big Dipper, the Little Dipper and Cassiopeia, over a three hour period.

As the sky turns, each star makes a circle around the pole. These circles are shown in the diagram, copied from a photograph taken by keeping the shutter of the camera open for several hours. Stars that are close to the pole make small circles, and can be seen all through the night. But stars that are far away from the pole are sometimes hidden by the ground. They rise in the east, pass over our heads, and then set in the west. In fact, as you watch the rising and setting of the stars, it becomes clear that the bowl of the sky is only half of a big sphere. The other half is always hidden by the ground. As the earth turns from west to east, this sphere seems to turn from east to west. As it turns, there are two points on the sphere that stand still. People who live in the northern hemisphere of the earth see only one of them, the north pole of the sky. People in the southern hemisphere see the south pole of the sky.

While the earth spins around once on its axis, the stars in the sky turn around once. That is why the amount of time it takes for the earth to make one full turn is called a star day, or *sidereal day*. The star day is divided into twenty-four star hours, which can be used to keep track of the position of a star. If we observe a star first when it is at the highest point of the circle it makes in the sky, we know it will then travel the full circle, or 360 degrees, in the next twenty four star hours. Since 360 divided by 24 gives 15, the star travels 15 degrees west in every star hour. Astronomers and navigators of ships and planes use this fact to help them find the positions of stars in the sky.

The Wanderers

While the stars look like spots of light pasted in place on the turning sky, the sun, the moon, and the planets behave very differently. They seem to move around among the stars as though they were bugs crawling around on the sphere of the sky. Because of this fact the ancient Greeks used to call them "the wanderers." They seem to move among the stars because of the different places they take as the earth and planets travel around the sun, and the moon travels around the earth.

The Short Rhythm Of The Sun—The Day

The rhythm of the sky that is easiest to see is the rhythm of the sun. The sun rises in the east and sets in the west, and then comes up again in the east once more. The amount of time it takes for a complete trip around is called the sun day, or *solar day*. Long ago people thought that the sun was really turning around the earth. But now we know that it only looks that way because the earth is spinning on its axis, and the movement of the sun that we see by day is like the movement of the stars that we see by night. But there is a slight difference, because the sun itself keeps changing its position among the stars.

To understand the way the sun changes its place among the stars, try this simple experiment. Put a chair in the middle of your room, and then look at it against the wall as a background. Now start walking around the chair. As you move, the chair will be seen against different parts of the wall as background. If you are moving to the right, the chair will shift to the left across the background of the walls. The sun shifts among the stars in the sky in the same way because the stars serve as the background while the earth moves around the sun just as you moved around your chair.

Because of this shifting of the sun against the background of the stars, it takes a little more than a star day for the sun to make a full round trip across the sky. The reason is shown in the diagram on page 26. In position 1, the boy sees the sun overhead. While the earth turns on its axis it also moves in its orbit around the sun, so that after one turn, or one star day, it will be in position 2. At that time the boy will find that the sun is not yet overhead. The earth must turn a little bit more, as shown by the large arrow in the

24

1

2

What you see
from Position 1

What you see
from Position 2

25

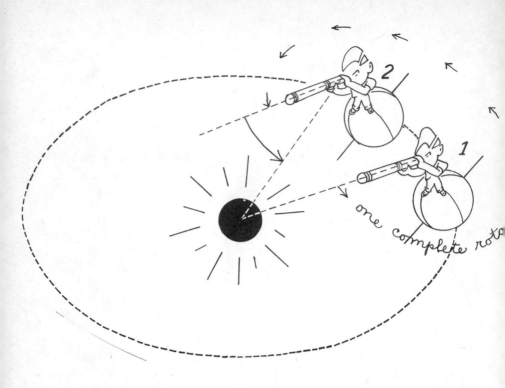

diagram, before he will see the sun overhead again. The time needed for this extra bit of turning is about 4 minutes.

We call the time between one noon and the next a sun day, or *solar day*. The solar day, as we see, is four minutes longer than the star day. The clock or watch you use every day is adjusted to keep solar time, so that twenty-four hours by your clock is the average length of the solar day.

The Long Rhythm Of The Sun—The Year

As the earth moves in its orbit around the sun, the sun is seen in a different position against the background of the stars from day to day. The sun seems to crawl among the

26

stars in a big circle, traveling almost one degree east each day. After 365¼ days it makes a complete round trip. The time taken for this round trip is called a year.

The yearly rhythm of the earth's motion around the sun shows itself in several ways. One of them is the changing position of the night sky. In the diagram you see the earth and the sun inside the sphere of stars that we seem to see when we look off into space in all directions. It is daytime for us when our part of the earth faces toward the sun. It is nighttime for us when our part of the earth faces away from the sun. The arrow on the left shows the direction in which we are looking when we face away from the sun to look at the stars overhead at midnight of a summer night. A half-year later, when the earth is on the other side of its orbit, the midnight sky is obviously in the opposite direction. If you look at the midnight sky from night to night, you find that each night it is turned one degree west. It takes a full year before it is turned back to its original position.

The rhythm of the earth's motion around the sun also

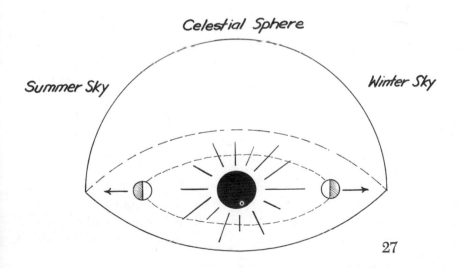

Celestial Sphere

Summer Sky

Winter Sky

shows itself in the sun's seeming to travel back and forth from north to south. This is the result of the fact that the earth's axis is tilted with respect to the plane of its orbit around the sun. The diagram below shows two opposite positions of the earth in its orbit. In one position, the north pole is tilted toward the sun, and the sun appears to be north of the equator. In the other position, the south pole is tilted toward the sun, and the sun appears to be south of the equator. The north-south motion of the sun in the sky accounts for the changing seasons from summer through fall to winter as the sun moves south, and back through spring to summer as the sun moves north again.

Summer   Winter

The Seasons

The Rhythm Of The Moon—The Month

The moon travels around the earth, so that when we look at the moon in the sky we see it moving against the background of the stars. Like the sun, it looks like a big lightning bug crawling around among the stars. If we see

28

the moon close to a certain star tonight, tomorrow night we will find it 13 degrees farther east, because it keeps moving steadily 13 degrees a day. It makes a complete trip, from star to star, coming back to the same part of the sky after $27\frac{1}{3}$ days.

The sun travels east across the sky at a speed of 1 degree a day. The moon travels east at a speed of 13 degrees a day. Because of the difference in the speeds with which they seem to move, they are like a hare and tortoise running a race around a circular track. The moon, starting from a place west of the sun, catches up with it at a speed of 12 degrees a day. Then it gets ahead of the sun, swings farther and farther east around the circle, and overtakes it again from the west. When the moon has just passed the sun, the time it takes to go all around the circle and pass the sun again is about $29\frac{1}{2}$ days. This amount of time is called a moon month, or *lunar month*.

The monthly rhythm of the moon shows itself in the sky in two ways. One way is in the movement of the moon toward and away from the sun as they race each other across the sky. When the moon and sun are on opposite sides of the sky, the moon is out only at night. But when the moon and sun are almost in the same direction from us, the moon seems close to the sun in the sky. Then the moon is out in the daytime, too. When the moon is west of the sun, the moon sets before the sun does. When the moon is east of the sun, it sets after the sun does.

The second way in which the rhythm of the moon shows itself is in the phases of the moon. The face of the moon isn't always fully lit up. When the moon seems close to the sun we see no light from the moon at all. Then as the moon moves east away from the sun, a patch of light begins to spread across the face of the moon from west to east, until,

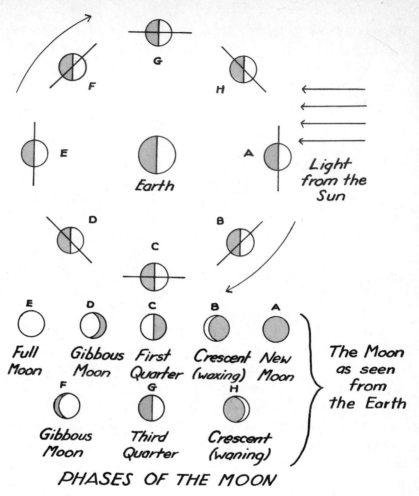

PHASES OF THE MOON

when the moon is on the opposite side of the sky from the sun, the full face of the moon is lit up. Then as the moon continues to move east, the patch of light shrinks, until, when the moon is back where it seems to be near the sun, we again see no more light from the moon.

These changes in phase of the moon arise from the fact that the moon does not give out its own light. It only reflects

30

to us the light that comes to it from the sun. For that reason, only that part of the moon is lit up that faces toward the sun. The rest of the moon is dark because it is in the moon's own shadow. When the part of the moon that is turned toward us is also facing the sun, we see the lit-up part. When the part of the moon that is turned toward us is facing away from the sun, we see the shadow. In in-between positions we see part light and part shadow. The diagram on page 30 shows how the moon passes from one phase to another.

The phase when the moon sends us no light at all is called the *new moon*. When the whole face is lit up, it is a *full moon*. When the lit-up part is becoming bigger, we say the moon is *waxing*. When it grows smaller we say the moon is *waning*.

Because of the fact that the lit-up part of the moon is the part that faces the sun, the horns of a crescent moon always point away from the sun. That is why the picture you see on this page, with the horns pointing toward the sun, is

What's wrong with this picture?

one that you could never see in the sky. Show the picture to your friends and ask them, "What's wrong with the picture?" It will be interesting to see how many wrong answers you get.

When the moon is "new" it has just passed the sun. As it continues to move eastward, away from the sun, it waxes. But since it is east of the sun, it will set after the sun does. Just before the moon passes the sun, it was west of the sun, and waning. But when the moon is west of the sun it sets before the sun does. Try this question on your friends and see how many get it right: When the moon sets shortly before the sun does, is it waxing or waning? You'll be surprised how many people who have seen the moon for years and years will never have noticed what the correct answer is.

The Tides

Another rhythm related to the moon is the rhythm of the tides. At any place at the seashore, the level of the sea rises and falls twice a day. The reason for this rhythm of the sea is shown in the diagram. The pull of the moon tends to separate the sea, at A, from the earth. This makes a

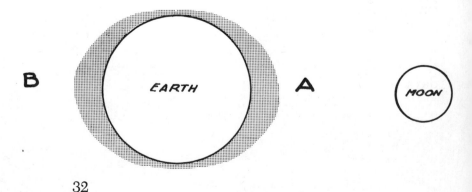

bulge in the sea, at A. The pull of the moon also tends to separate the earth from the sea at B. This makes another bulge in the sea, at B. Since the earth rotates, different parts of it keep moving into the positions where the bulges are formed. So the high-tide bulges travel around the earth once a day. Because there are two of them, each place has high tide twice a day.

In the moon's eastward motion across the sky, it gains on the sun at the rate of about 12 degrees a day. The earth turns about 12 degrees in 50 minutes. That is why high tide comes 50 minutes later each day.

The Day, And Groups Of Days

Of all the rhythms in the sky, the one that we are bound to notice first is the daily rising and setting of the sun. Not only do we see this rhythm in the way day follows night and night follows day. We also *live* this rhythm because we sleep by night and are awake by day. That is why it is natural for us to measure time by counting days.

When we measure long periods of time by counting days, it is necessary to use large numbers. We can avoid the large numbers by counting groups of days. For example, 90 days can be divided into 3 groups of 30 days each, or 3 months. Also, 730 days can be divided into two groups of 365 days each, or 2 years. That is why we use all three rhythms of the sky together, and measure time in years, months, and days.

For periods of time shorter than a month it is convenient to use a smaller group of days. This smaller group is the *week*. While the day, month, and year are based on a natural rhythm of the sky, the week is not. The ancient Chinese had a week of five days, named after the five elements that were thought to be the building blocks of the world: iron, wood, water, feathers, and earth. Jews, Christians, and Mohammedans use a week of seven days. The seven-day week plays an important part in their religions, because in the story of the Creation, God is said to have made the world in six days and rested on the seventh. This is the reason they give for using one day out of seven as a day of rest.

We do not know just why seven was chosen for the number of days of the week. Some people think it is because seven was thought to be a magic number in many old beliefs. Others think it was chosen because there were seven wanderers that the people could see in the sky: the sun, the moon, and the planets Mercury, Venus, Mars, Jupiter, and Saturn. This theory is partly supported by the names of the days of the week:

Sunday is Sun-day.

Monday is Moon-day.

Tuesday is Tiw's day, named after the god Tiw, Old English name for Mars.

Wednesday is Woden's day, named after the god Woden, Old English name for Mercury.

Thursday is Thor's day, named after the god Thor, another name for Jupiter.

Friday is Frig's day, named after the goddess Frig, Old English name for Venus.

Saturday is Saturn-day.

CHAPTER III

The Calendar

Matching Rhythms

OVER two thousand years ago people were already using four rhythms to measure time: the daily rhythm of the rising and setting of the sun, the weekly rhythm of groups of seven days, the monthly rhythm of the phases of the moon, and the yearly rhythm of the changing seasons. When they tried to match these rhythms they got what we call a *calendar* which fits days and weeks into months; and months into years.

What should an ideal calendar be like? First, the rhythm of the years should match exactly the rhythm of the seasons, so that the same season always comes in the same part of a year. This is necessary if the calendar is to help us know when to expect spring, summer, fall, and winter. It is especially important for the farmer who must know when to plant his seeds, and when to gather the harvest. Secondly, the year should be divided into a whole number of months, so that a new year always begins with a new month. Third, the month should be divided into a whole number of days, so that a new month always begins with a new day and not in the middle of a day. Fourth, the rhythm of the months should match the phases of the moon, so that the same phase of the moon always comes in the same part of a

35

month. Fifth, all years should be the same length, and all months should be the same length.

It wasn't long before people found out that they couldn't have this kind of calendar. Since the phases of the moon have a rhythm of 29½ days, a month with a whole number of days will not match the rhythm. If all months are made 29 days, the month will be too short, and the new moon phase will come later and later each month. If all months are made 30 days, the month will be too long, and the new moon will come earlier and earlier each month. One way of avoiding this trouble is to give up the idea of having equal months and to alternate 29-day months with 30-day months. In this way the phases of the moon are almost perfectly matched with the days of the month.

But if we fit the months to the phases of the moon, it solves one problem yet creates another, because no whole number of lunar months can be fitted into a year. If we alternate 29-day months with 30-day months the average month is 29½ days. Twelve of these would add up to 354 days, which is 11¼ days short of a full year. If we want the years to match the rhythm of the sun that appears in the rhythm of the seasons, then the months can't match the rhythm of the moon. If we want the months to match the rhythm of the moon, then the years can't match the rhythm of the sun. That's why people had to choose either the moon or the sun as the basis of their calendar.

A Moon Calendar

The ancient Hebrews chose the moon. They wanted each month to begin at the time of the new moon. To make this possible they had to give up the idea of having equal years. They let most years have twelve months, and then made up for the missing 11¼ days by putting in a thirteenth month every three years. Other special rules make the Hebrew calendar a rather complicated one.

A Sun Calendar

The ancient Romans chose the sun. But even they ran into trouble, because the rhythm of the seasons takes 365¼ days. No whole number of days will fit it exactly. Because of this kind of poor fit, the Roman calendar in the days of Julius Caesar had gotten three months out of step with the rhythm of the sun. Caesar corrected this difficulty in the 46th year B.C. by introducing a streamlined calendar. To make the average length of a year 365¼ days, he set the length of a year at 365 days, except that every fourth year would be a leap year with 366 days. He gave 31 days each to the odd-numbered months January, March, May, July, September, and November. He gave 30 days each to all the rest, except February, which got 29 days for normal years and 30 days for a leap year.

Before he made these changes the year began in March. September, October, November, and December were number names in Latin meaning seventh, eighth, ninth, and tenth month, respectively. But Caesar moved the beginning of the year to January, so the names of these months don't match their numbers any more. To honor Caesar, the new-style seventh month was given his name. That's why it is now called July (after Julius).

The Jealous Emperor

More changes were made in the calendar later by the Emperor Augustus. The eighth month was named in his

37

honor, so now we call it August. Under Julius Caesar's rules this month had only 30 days, while July had 31. Augustus thought he was just as important as his uncle Julius, so why shouldn't his month have 31 days too? So he took a day from February and gave it to August. Then, to avoid having three months in a row with 31 days, he cut September and November to 30 days, and raised October and December to 31. Julius Caesar's calendar, as changed by Augustus, was used for hundreds of years, and is known as the *Julian Calendar*.

Ten Days That Were Lost

The Julian Calendar had its troubles, too. It would have been all right if a year were exactly 365¼ days long. But actually it is 365 days 5 hours 48 minutes and 46 seconds long. The small mistake of 11 minutes 14 seconds per year doesn't seem like much, but when it piles up for hundreds of years it becomes a big mistake. By the year 1582 the calendar was 10 days behind where it should have been. This new problem was solved by Pope Gregory XIII, who boldly abolished ten days from the calendar, calling the day after October 4, 1582, October 15th.

The mistake in the Julian Calendar was found to be 3 days every 400 years. To be sure that it didn't start building up again, Pope Gregory also ordered that we leave out the 29th day of February in every year that can be divided by 100, unless it can be divided by 400. That is why the years 1700, 1800, and 1900 were not leap years, but the year 2000 will be.

The calendar of Pope Gregory is known as the *Gregorian Calendar*. It was adopted by Spain, Portugal, and part

of Italy on October 15, 1582. Other countries began using it at later dates. England and its American colonies adopted it on September 14, 1752. Russia adopted it February 14, 1918. But the Greek Orthodox Church still uses the Julian Calendar, now 13 days behind the Gregorian Calendar, and so it celebrates Christmas 13 days after the Roman Catholic and Protestant Churches do.

Should We Change The Calendar Again?

Since the changes made by Pope Gregory, the calendar has not been tampered with to the present day. But some people are still worried about it. Astronomers tell us that the Gregorian year is 26 seconds too long. This mistake will add up to a whole day in 3,323 years. To wipe out this mistake they suggest that we leave out the 29th day of February in each year that can be divided by 4000. Obviously we don't have to hurry in making up our minds about this suggestion. If our descendants who live in the year 4000 decide to carry it out, then the calendar after that would not be more than a day wrong for twenty thousand years. That should be accurate enough to please the fussiest people.

Another kind of change has been suggested by the members of the World Calendar Association. They want every month to start on Sunday and be exactly four weeks long. So they propose that we divide the year into 13 months of 28 days each. This takes care of only 364 days. The left-over day they would call New Year's Day and put it into no month at all. In leap years they would have us observe two New Years Days. Under this calendar your birthday would always fall on the same day of the week.

A Perpetual Calendar

When you divide 365 days into weeks, you get 52 weeks, with one day left over. So in the Gregorian Calendar, if a year begins on Monday, and it is not a leap year, the next year begins on Tuesday. But if it is a leap year, the next year begins on Wednesday. That is why we need a new calendar each year.

If you are tired of changing your calendar each year, you can use a perpetual calendar, one that is good for every year. Here are directions for making one that will be good up to the year 1999.

40

Trace the diagram on the next page on a clean sheet of paper. Then, on the traced copy, cut along the two horizontal lines ABCD, and the vertical lines AA, BB, CC, and DD. This will separate from the rest of the sheet the three pieces of the perpetual calendar. Now rest the largest piece on a newspaper lying flat on the table, and with a razor cut along the dotted lines printed on it. Be careful not to cut beyond the dotted lines. The boxes marked "cut out" will be removed altogether. In addition you will be cutting slits marked EE, FF, GG, and HH. Now insert the narrow strips through the slits, as shown in the picture marked with the heavy arrow, and your perpetual calendar is ready to use. Slide the upper strip until the letter Y is under the year you want. (If you want 1960, put the Y under the column in which "60" appears.) Then slide the lower strip until the letter M is under the month you want. Then the bottom cutout will show you the calendar for that month. Notice that there are two different settings for leap years, one to be used before March 1st, the other to be used after February 29th. This calendar always shows 31 days in a month; for the shorter months simply disregard the extra days.

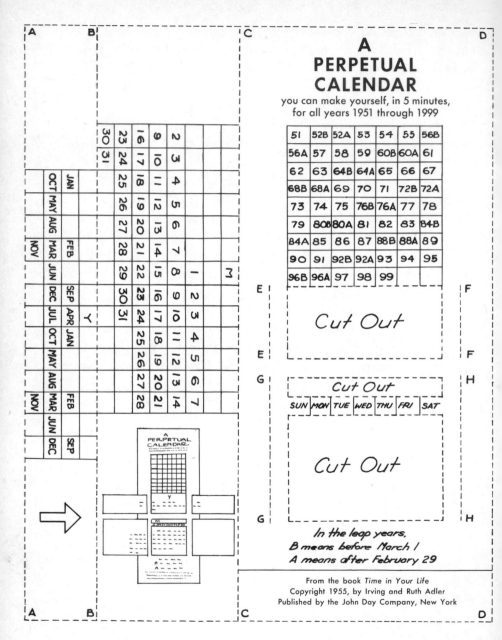

A PERPETUAL CALENDAR

you can make yourself, in 5 minutes,
for all years 1951 through 1999

51	52B	52A	53	54	55	56B
56A	57	58	59	60B	60A	61
62	63	64B	64A	65	66	67
68B	68A	69	70	71	72B	72A
73	74	75	76B	76A	77	78
79	80B	80A	81	82	83	84B
84A	85	86	87	88B	88A	89
90	91	92B	92A	93	94	95
96B	96A	97	98	99		

Cut Out

Cut Out

SUN	MON	TUE	WED	THU	FRI	SAT

Cut Out

*In the leap years,
B means before March 1
A means after February 29*

From the book *Time in Your Life*
Copyright 1955, by Irving and Ruth Adler
Published by the John Day Company, New York

CHAPTER IV

Sky Clocks

TO measure lengths of time that are less than a day we use clocks and watches. But thousands of years ago, before such clocks were invented, people knew how to tell time anyhow. How would *you* tell time if you didn't have a watch or clock to look at? If you are outdoors on a clear night, you don't need your watch to show you the time. Simply look up at the sky. The whole sky is turning steadily, and you can tell time by the changing position of the stars, the way people did thousands of years ago.

Telling Time By The Stars

To tell time by the stars, first face north and look for the Big Dipper and Cassiopeia. The pointers of the Big Dipper help you find Polaris, which is about halfway between the Big Dipper and Cassiopeia. Polaris is the center of the star clock, and the Dipper and Cassiopeia turn around it. Imagine a line drawn from Polaris to Caph, one of the bright stars of Cassiopeia. (See the diagram on page 45.) This line will be the hour hand of the star clock, pointing out the time.

43

The Face Of The Star Clock

The face of an ordinary clock is divided into 12 hours. And when the hour hand moves away from the 12, it moves to the right. The face of the star clock is different. Since the sky makes one complete turn in a day, the face of the star clock is divided into 24 hours. A quarter of a turn takes 6 hours. Also, the stars don't turn the way the hands of an ordinary clock do. They turn in the opposite direction, or counterclockwise.

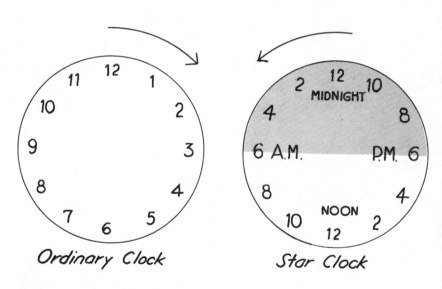

Ordinary Clock   Star Clock

The Time On September 21st

First we will learn to read the star clock on September 21st. On that day, the hour hand of the star clock points straight up at 12 midnight. Before midnight it will be to the right or east of the midnight position. After midnight it will be to the left or west of the midnight position.

The diagrams show the appearance of the sky at 9 P.M., 12 midnight, and 3 A.M. on that day.

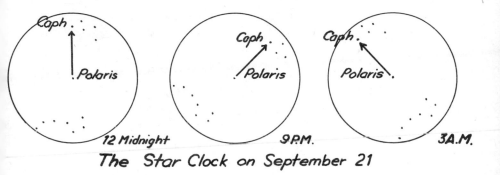

The Star Clock on September 21

To find the time for any position of the sky, first locate the hour hand, the line from Polaris to Caph. Then esti mate how many hours of turning separate it from the midnight position. To be able to do this accurately, practice dividing the sky into hours in this way: Imagine two lines drawn through Polaris, one going straight up, and the other a level line going to the right. The lines will form an angle of 90 degrees, and will include one quarter

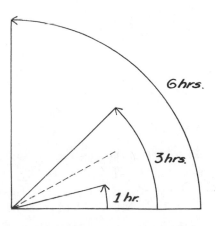

45

of the sky. This represents 6 hours of turning. Now imagine the 90-degree angle cut in half. Each half represents 3 hours of turning. Now imagine each half divided into 3 equal parts. Each part will represent one hour of turning. In the same way, you can divide each of the other quarters of the sky into 6 equal hours.

Now, for practice, let's read the time shown by diagrams A and B. In diagram A, the hour hand is four hours after its midnight position. On September 21st, this would mean 4 A.M. In diagram B, the hour hand is two hours before its midnight position. On September 21st this would show the time as 10 P.M.

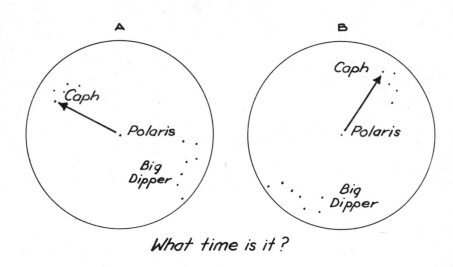

What time is it?

Star Time Any Day Of The Year

The star clock, as we have read it so far, tells the right time on September 21st. But it tells the wrong time on every other day of the year. This is because our calendar

46

keeps track of solar days, and the solar day is longer than the star day. (See page 26.) Because of this difference, the turning of the stars is faster than the passing of the ordinary day. So the star clock is a clock that runs too fast. It gains 4 minutes every day. In a week it gains 28 minutes, which is about a half-hour. In a month it gains about 2 hours. But, as long as we know how much it gains, we can still use it to tell time for any day of the year. All we have to do is make a correction of 2 hours for every month, or a half-hour for every week, between that day and September 21st. The correction is subtracted for time after September 21st. It is added for time before September 21st.

Let's practice, now, by reading the time from the diagrams below. In diagram *A*, the hour hand of the clock shows 12 midnight. But November 21st is two months after September 21st. The correction is 4 hours to be subtracted, and the correct time is 8 P.M.

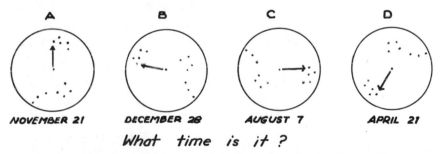

NOVEMBER 21   DECEMBER 28   AUGUST 7   APRIL 21

What time is it ?

In diagram *B*, the hour hand of the clock shows 5 A.M. But December 28th is three months and one week after September 21st. The correction is 6½ hours to be subtracted, and the correct time is 10:30 P.M.

In diagram *C*, the hour hand of the clock shows 6 P.M. But August 7th is one month and two weeks before Sep-

47

tember 21st. The correction is 3 hours to be added, and the correct time is 9 P.M. In diagram D, the hour hand of the clock shows 10 A.M. But April 21st is five months before September 21st. The correction is 10 hours to be added, and the correct time is 8 P.M.

For directions for making an automatic star clock, see page 128.

The Sundial

In the daytime the bright light of the sun, scattered by the air, outshines the feeble light of the stars and hides them. So, while the star clock keeps turning in the daytime, we can't see it, and have to tell time in another way.

One way would be to watch the changing position of the sun itself, because it, too, can serve as the hand of a clock. It travels along a circle, from east to west, going 15 degrees an hour. When it is highest in the sky, the time is 12 noon. But the sun clock is not as easy to read as the star clock. Since we can't see Polaris in the daytime, we don't see the center around which the sun turns with the sky. Also, the sun doesn't travel on the same circle each day. With approaching winter the circle moves to the south, and with approaching summer it moves back up north. For both of these reasons, it is difficult to judge how much the sky has turned by merely comparing the positions of the sun.

Thousands of years ago people got around these difficulties by inventing the sundial. A sundial is simply a stick that casts a shadow. As the sun moves across the sky, the

48

shadow turns, and points out the time like the hour hand of a clock.

Making a sundial would be easy for someone living at the North Pole. If he drove a vertical stick into the ice right above the Pole, the stick would point along the axis of the earth. As the earth spun on its axis, the sun would travel in a circle around this stick. Meanwhile, the shadow the stick cast on the ground, always pointing away from the sun, would travel around in a circle at the same time. Since it would make one complete turn in 24 hours, it would travel 15 degrees in one hour.

Although we don't live at the North Pole, we, too, can use this simple North Pole design. All we have to do is place our sundial so that its stick points in the same direction as the earth's axis. And we must catch the shadow, not on the ground, but on a flat surface parallel to the ground at the North Pole. Here are directions for making and setting up this kind of sundial.

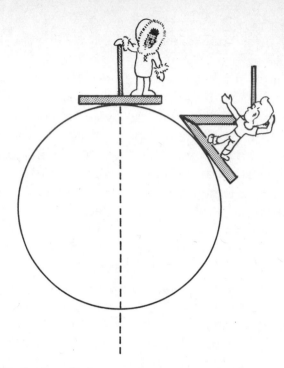

A Home-Made Sundial

First look up your latitude in an atlas. Then subtract it from 90 degrees. Now, cut two wedge-shaped pieces of wood with the angle of each wedge equal to the result. For example, if your latitude is 42 degrees, you subtract it from 90 degrees, and make the wedges 48 degrees. (Diagram A.) Now cut out two rectangular boards about 12 by 18 inches. On one board, draw a line parallel to the long edge, 1 inch from the long edge. (Diagram B.) Through the center of this line, nail a 4-inch-long dowel at right angles to the board. Divide the space above the line into 12 angles of 15 degrees each, with the aid of a protractor. (Diagram C.) Label these angle lines from 6 A.M. to 6 P.M. as shown in the diagram. Now nail the two boards

50

to the wedges so that the boards touch at one edge, and the hour lines on the upper board point away from the free edge, as shown in the diagram. Your sundial is now complete. But, before you can use it, you must set it up in the proper position. The bottom board has to be level. The edge where the two boards meet must run east and west. To level the bottom board, use a carpenter's level. The east-west line is, of course, at right angles to the north-south line. To locate north, use one of the methods described in the next paragraph. When the sundial is correctly set up, the dowel is parallel to the earth's axis, the upper board is parallel to the ground at the North Pole, and the shadow of the dowel points out the time.

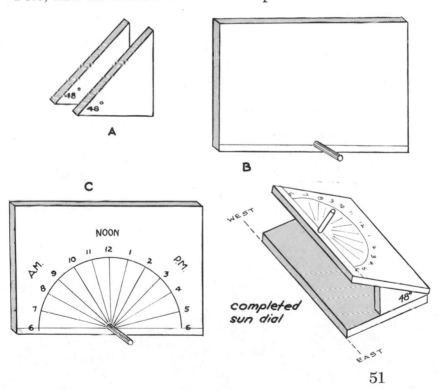

A

B

C

NOON

12
10 11   1
9   2
A.M.   P.M.
8   3
7   4
6   5
6

WEST

EAST

48°

completed
sun dial

51

How To Find North

There are several easy ways of finding north.

On a clear night you can locate north by looking for Polaris. If you face Polaris, a line on the ground in the direction in which you are facing will be a north-south line.

In the daytime you can't see Polaris. But then you can locate north from the position of the sun. If you have a watch to help you, you can do it in this way: Hold your watch level, and place a thin twig, held straight up, over the center of the face of the watch. Now turn the watch until the hour hand coincides with the shadow of the twig. North will be halfway between the shadow and the 12.

If you have no watch, you can use the shadow of a stick in another way. Drive a stick vertically into the ground. As the sun crosses the sky in the course of the day, the shadow of the stick will turn. It will also grow shorter in the morning, and longer again in the afternoon. When the shadow is shortest, at noon, it will point north.

Another more accurate method requires watching the

length of the shadow for a longer time. Draw a circle on the ground, using the vertical stick as center. You can make the circle by tying one end of a rope around the stick, and knotting the other end to a small twig. Then, while pulling the rope tight, swing the extended rope around the center stick and scratch a full circle on the ground with the twig, in the same way that you use compasses. If the circle is not made too small, the end of the shadow of the center stick will be outside the circle in the morning and afternoon, and inside the circle during the middle of the day. There will be two instants when the end of the shadow will be right on the circle. Watch for these instants, and draw lines where the shadow rests on the ground. North will be halfway between these two lines.

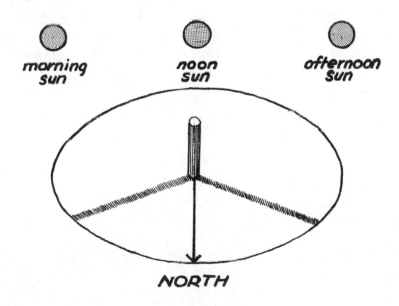

CHAPTER V

Man-Made Clocks

THE sundial took timekeeping out of the sky and put it down on the ground. It was one of the earliest of the man-made clocks, known to the ancient Egyptians and other peoples of Africa and Asia. Several different types were invented, more complicated than the home-made sundial described in the last chapter. The ancient Greeks learned about the sundial from their eastern neighbors. The Romans got it from the Greeks and passed it on to the rest of Europe. From Europe it crossed the Atlantic Ocean to the Americas. Today we still find sundials used as decorations in public parks.

The Water Clock

The sundial has one great disadvantage as a daytime clock. It doesn't work when the sun is hidden by clouds. In order to be able to keep track of time day or night, rain or shine, it was necessary to make clocks that had nothing to do with the movement of the sky. This problem was solved in ancient Egypt by the invention of the water clock, the first all-weather timepiece.

In its simplest form the water clock is a bowl filled with water which is allowed to empty out through a hole near

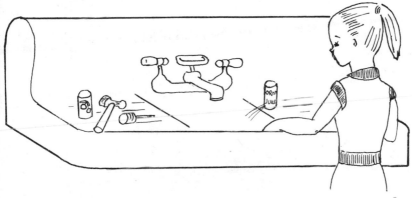

the base. It serves as a timekeeper because it always takes
the same amount of time to empty the bowl. In the courts
of ancient Athens, when a citizen spoke to the judges, a
court attendant used the water clock, called a clepsydra,
to make sure he didn't talk too long. The court attendant
was kept busy all day refilling the bowl.

Three thousand years ago the Emperor of China had
another kind of water clock that worked in reverse. Instead of emptying out, his clock filled up. He used a bowl
with a hole in the bottom and floated it in a basin of water.
The bowl gradually filled with water until it sank to the
bottom of the basin.

You can make a water clock of your own from a tin can
that is open at the top. With an awl make a hole in the
side of the can, near the bottom. Hold your finger over
the hole while you fill the can with water. Remove your
finger, and allow the can to empty into the sink or a bowl.

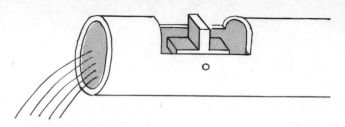

The higher you punch the hole, the less time it will take for the water to stop flowing. If you make several water clocks with the hole punched at different heights from the bottom, you can find the correct height for making a three minute egg-timer.

More complicated water clocks were made by allowing water to flow in and out of a container at the same time. A steady flow of water was used to mark the steady flow of time by turning a dial.

This was made possible by using a water wheel with vanes on it, as in the diagram. The wheel was placed in a pipe through which the water flowed. The water, pushing its way through the pipe, pressed against the vane that

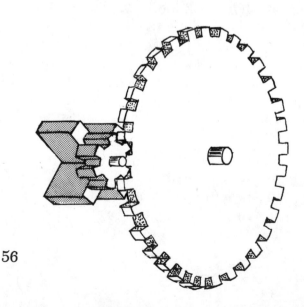

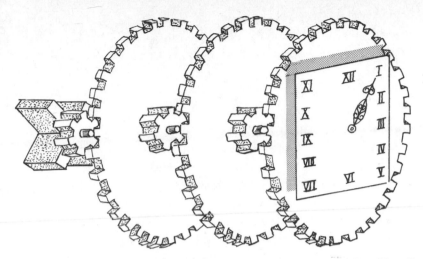

reached into the pipe. As the vane was pushed, the wheel turned, and the next vane dipped into the water, to be pushed in turn.

Turning The Hand

On the usual clock face, the hour hand makes only one complete turn in twelve hours. The water wheel turned much faster, making thousands of turns in that time. To use the turning of the water wheel to turn the hands of the clock, it was necessary to have a way of changing fast turning into slow turning. This was done by the use of gears. A small pinion with a few teeth was placed on the axle of the water wheel. This pinion was meshed with a large wheel that had many teeth. When the small pinion made one complete turn, the large wheel turned only part way. So it took many turns of the pinion to make the wheel turn around once. In this way the fast turning of the pinion was changed into the slow turning of the wheel.

Another small pinion was placed on the axle of the large

wheel, and meshed with a second large wheel. Each time the first large wheel turned once, the small pinion on its axle also turned once, and made the second large wheel turn only part way. In this way the turning was slowed down even more. A train of several gears, arranged as shown in the diagram, was used to make the very slow turning needed for the hand of the clock. The water wheel was attached to the first pinion in the train, and the hour hand was attached to the last wheel in the train. Gear trains are used in modern clocks, too, but they are used in reverse to change slow turning into fast turning.

In some of the old water clocks the power of the moving water was also used to ring bells and move little figures. In the year 809, Harun Al-Rashid, the Caliph of Bagdad, sent a marvelous water clock to Charlemagne, king of the Franks. This clock showed the time on a clock face, rang a bell every hour, and made the figures of horsemen ride out of a door and back again at 12 o'clock.

The Hour Glass

One trouble with the water clock was that it might freeze in cold weather. A French monk in the eighth century avoided this trouble by using sand instead of water, making the first hour glass. In an hour glass, two glass funnels are joined at their narrow ends, one above the other, and mounted between wooden plates. Time is measured by the flow of sand from the upper funnel, through the narrow connecting passage, into the lower funnel. When all the sand is in the bottom funnel, the glass is turned upside down to start the flow over again. Small three-minute glasses can be bought today to serve as egg-timers.

The Clock That Burns Up

Another clock used in the Middle Ages was the candle clock. When a candle of uniform thickness burns, it grows shorter at a steady rate. So the length of the burning candle can be used to mark the passage of time.

You can make a simple candle clock yourself. Light an ordinary paraffin candle that is the same thickness through its whole length, and allow it to burn for a half-hour. Then compare it with another candle of the same kind to see what length of the candle was burned up. Now divide the candle into equal sections of this length. You can mark the sections easily by tying dark thread around the candle. Make a slipknot with the thread and loop it around the candle at the end of each section. Pull the knot tight until the thread cuts into the candle, so it won't slip from place. Now when the candle is lit you will know that every time another section has burned up, another half-hour has passed.

The Fragrant Clock

The candle clock gives you light while it keeps time. The Chinese developed a clock that combines timekeeping with sweet odors. This is the incense stick, or joss stick as it is sometimes called. The stick is made of clay mixed with the sawdust of fragrant woods. It is burned in connection with religious observances. The stick rests on a plate, and burns slowly. The smoke carries the fragrant odors into the air. At the same time the burning stick, like a candle clock, shows the passage of time by the length of the part that has burned up.

The joss stick clock has been used as an alarm clock, too. Two metal balls are tied to a thread that is placed across a burning joss stick. The metal balls hang down over a metal plate. As time passes, the burning end of the stick creeps closer to the thread. When it burns through the thread, the balls fall down and strike the plate below, making it ring like a bell.

The Modern Clock

The water clock that could turn a dial was the ancestor of the modern clock. It already had the main features that are found in every modern clock: a source of *power* to make the hands move; a *regulator* to keep them moving at an even rate; and a *gear train* to change the speed of turning. The power was supplied by falling water. The reservoir from which the water flowed was kept filled to the same level all the time. This kept the pressure steady and assured an even rate of flow. The gear train changed the fast turning of the water wheel into the slow turning of the hand that pointed out the time. The modern clock developed from the water clock as people learned to use new sources of power to move the hands, and new ways to make sure that they moved at a steady rate.

The Power Behind The Hand

In a water clock the power came from falling water. Archimedes, who lived over two thousand years ago, was the first to think of using a falling weight instead. In a weight-driven clock one end of a cord is tied to the weight, and the other end is attached to an axle. Then the cord is wound up on the axle, like thread on a spool. When the weight falls, the cord unwinds, and the axle is made to turn. A gear train connects the axle to several wheels. As the axle turns, the wheels turn at different speeds. The regulator described on page 66 controls the turning of the fastest of these wheels. Two of the slower wheels turn the hands on the face of the clock. Only a few years ago people still had wall clocks that got their power in this way. Now you are more likely to see such a clock in a museum than in a home.

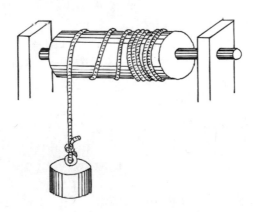

A clock that got its power from a falling weight had to stay in one place. Clocks that could be carried around became possible when the falling weight was replaced by a coiled spring. This was first done in the year 1480 by Peter Henlein, a young German locksmith who lived in Nuremberg. Henlein's portable clocks, the ancestors of modern watches, were called "Nuremberg Eggs" because of their shape.

A spring is a stubborn thing. When you wind it up, it tries to unwind again. So when you wind it you are storing power in it, and the spring releases the power as it unwinds. The spring that supplies the power for a watch or clock is called the *main spring*. The main spring is coiled inside a little metal barrel. The inner end of the spring is attached to a metal rod that doesn't move. The outer end is attached to the inside of the barrel. When you wind up a watch, you are turning the barrel. As the barrel is turned, the coils of the spring are tightened. When you stop winding it, the spring begins to unwind. This makes the barrel turn back again. The turning of the barrel drives the gear train in the watch.

The modern electric clock uses neither weights nor springs for power. An electric current supplies the power to make a small electric motor turn. The usual gear train connects the motor to the hands of the clock.

Giving The Clock Rhythm

It takes more than a power supply to keep a clock moving so it can measure time. You can see why this is so by trying a simple experiment. Borrow your mother's spool of button thread, and tie a weight (a metal nut or washer will do) to the end of the thread. Slip the spool over a knitting needle held level, and allow the weight to fall. It will fall quickly to the floor, and, as the thread unwinds, the spool will turn. In less than two seconds the whole action is over. If the turning of the spool were used to turn the hands of a clock, the hands would whirl around quickly for a short time and then stop. Such a "clock" would be of little help as a timepiece. The falling weight does its work well in supplying power, but it gives you the power too fast.

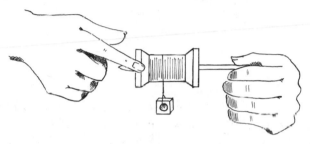

Now wind the thread back on the spool and get ready to drop the weight again. This time, as the weight falls, tap the edge of the spool with your finger, using a rapid rhythm. Your finger will act like a brake, and each tap will stop the spool. The weight will fall in small jerks, with a regular rhythm. The turning of the spool will not be smooth, but *it will be slow and steady.* The power of the falling weight is now under control, and you can measure time by the rhythm of the spool.

This experiment shows you why a regulator is needed in a clock. The regulator is a brake with a built-in rhythm. By serving as a brake that goes on and off it slows down the delivery of the power of the clock and keeps it under control. By its rhythm it marks off equal intervals of time that can be counted to measure the passage of time.

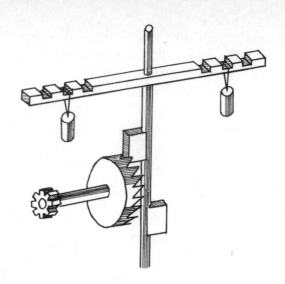

The first practical regulator for use in a weight-driven clock was invented by Pope Sylvester in the year 996. It had two main parts, the *escape wheel,* and the *balance.* The escape wheel was like the turning spool in your experiment, but it had teeth. The balance had two fingers which took turns at stopping the wheel. The diagram shows the upper finger stopping the wheel by resting between two teeth. But the stopping lasted only a moment. The wheel, forced to turn by the falling weight, pushed the finger around out of the way. This made the whole balance swing halfway around, and then the lower finger landed between two teeth and stopped the wheel. The lower finger was then pushed out of the way, and so the balance kept turning, stopping the wheel at each half-turn. The weights hanging from the crosspiece of the balance made it heavier and harder to turn, so the wheel would not go too fast. This type of escape wheel and balance was used in both wall clocks and Nuremberg Eggs.

Improving The Rhythm

There was one weakness of the escape wheel and balance combination. Its rhythm was the rhythm of the turning of the balance. And this rhythm was not very regular. The turns between stops didn't always take exactly the same amount of time. So, while clocks built with the balance were practical, they weren't very accurate. They had to be reset often by checking them against a sundial or the stars. To build more accurate clocks it was necessary, first, to find a regulator with a regular rhythm.

A better regulator became possible when the great scientist Galileo discovered the law of the pendulum in 1564. He made his discovery, we are told, as he watched the swinging of the great lamp that hung in the Cathedral of Pisa. You can see what Galileo saw by performing this simple experiment. To make a pendulum, tie a small weight to a string, and let it hang down as you hold the other end of the string between your fingers. Now pull the weight to a side and release it. It will begin swinging back and forth. You will notice that *each swing takes the same amount of time*. If you make the string shorter, the pendulum will swing faster, but still with a regular rhythm.

Galileo's discovery that the pendulum has a regular rhythm meant that it could be used as a regulator. However, a hundred years went by before it was used that way,

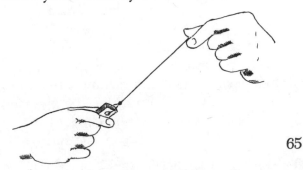

when the first pendulum clock was made by the Dutch scientist Christian Huyghens. In the pendulum clock, a balance lever with two fingers is fastened across the top of the pendulum. As the pendulum swings back and forth, first one finger, and then the other, is poked between the teeth of the escape wheel and stops it. The push that the escape wheel gives to the fingers keeps the pendulum swinging wide without dying down.

The Rhythm Of The Hog's Hair

While the pendulum improved the wall clock, it did nothing to help the watch, because you can't have a swinging pendulum in something you carry around in your pocket. But the watch, too, got a better regulator when the English scientist Robert Hooke found that a vibrating spring has a regular rhythm. In 1685 he built a watch that used as a regulator a coiled spring made of hog's hair. Though watch regulators are now made of metal, they are still called *hair springs.*

In the modern watch, a coiled hair spring is mounted inside a small wheel known as the *balance wheel.* One end of the spring is fastened to the frame of the watch, and the other end to the shaft of the wheel. When the wheel is given a push, it turns, and tightens the coils of the spring. The spring pushes back, slows down the turning of the wheel, stops it, and starts it turning the other way. As the wheel turns back, its own motion carries it past its starting position, and again puts a strain on the spring. So again the spring slows the wheel, stops it, and pushes it the other way. In this way the balance wheel swings back and forth, keeping the regular rhythm of the vibrating spring. A lever with two fingers is attached to the balance wheel and swings with it. The fingers stop the teeth of the escape wheel just as they do in the pendulum clock.

Remote Control

An electric clock has no pendulum or hair spring. It has a regulator that you cannot see, because it isn't in the clock at all. The rhythm that regulates the electric clock is the rhythm of the alternating current that feeds it. The current is regulated in the power house by controlling the speed of the dynamos that make it. The common electric clock is designed to use an electric current that goes back and forth in the wires 60 times a second (60-cycle alternating current). Each time the current goes back and forth once, the little electric motor in the clock turns around once. So the motor turns 60 times a second, or 3,600 times a minute. The gear train changes this high speed into the slow turning of the hands of the clock face.

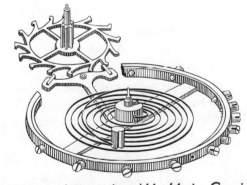

Balance Wheel with Hair Spring

CHAPTER VI

Time Around the World

Local Time

BECAUSE most people do their work in the day-time, when the sun is out, it would be natural that they set their clocks to give them solar time. In solar time it is noon for you when the sun is directly over the meridian or north-south line through your place on the ground. But then it will not be noon for anybody who is east or west of your position. Because the earth turns from west to east, a meridian east of you has already passed under the sun and so has had its noon earlier. A meridian west of you has not yet passed under the sun and so will have its noon later. Because of this effect of the turning of the earth, all places on the same meridian have the same solar time, and all places on different meridians have different solar times. Because solar time can be different from place to place it is also called *local time.*

The separation of two meridians is measured in degrees of longitude. Because the earth turns 15 degrees an hour, the difference in time between two meridians is one hour for every 15 degrees of longitude. At the latitude of Chicago it is one minute for every thirteen miles, or one second for every 1,140 feet of distance east or west.

Imagine what life would be like if all people used local

time. Suppose you lived at the western end of Chicago and made an appointment to visit a friend at the eastern end. If you kept the appointment by your watch, you would be 67 seconds late by your friend's watch, because that's how much the time differs between the two ends. If you wanted to have the right time always, you'd have to move your watch ahead or back every time you moved east or west. In New York you'd have to move your watch 5 seconds if you merely walked across the Brooklyn Bridge!

Standard Time

To avoid this trouble, people within a city or town agreed to use only one time, so that all clocks in the town would agree. This was helpful as long as people stayed in the town. But when they began to travel greater distances, especially after railroads were built, they had the same trouble all over again. Every town west or east had a different

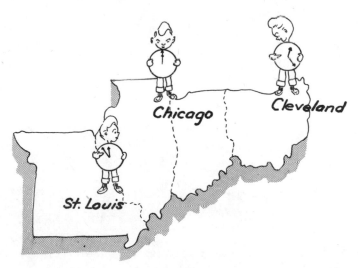

St. Louis

Chicago

Cleveland

time. When it was noon in Chicago it was 12:24 in Cleveland and 11:50 in St. Louis. The only way to avoid confusion was to have people in large regions use the same *standard time*.

In England, in 1848, the time at Greenwich, where the naval observatory is located, became the standard for the whole country. In the United States and Canada the railroads introduced standard time on November 18, 1883. They divided the North American continent into five zones, approximately 15 degrees wide. Each zone has one standard time, which differs from the time of the next zone east or west by one hour. The zones, going from east to west, are Atlantic, Eastern, Central, Mountain, and Pacific. The eastern part of Canada lies in the Atlantic zone. However,

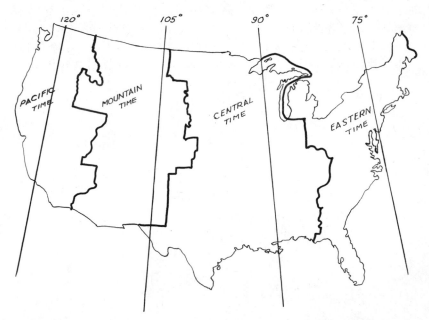

Standard Time Zones in the United States

no part of the United States is in it. The local time of the 60th meridian is the standard for the Atlantic zone. The local time of the 75th meridian is the standard for the Eastern zone. The Central, Mountain, and Pacific zones use the times of the 90th, 105th, and 120th meridians.

The Day Of Two Noons

The day that standard time went into effect in the United States and Canada many places had two noons. In the eastern zone, for example, the new time began when it was noon by local time at the 75th meridian, and the time of this meridian became the standard for the whole zone. Any town east of this meridian had had its own local noon earlier. When the town shifted to standard time it went back to noon again. So that day such a town had two noons.

Twenty-Five Hours A Day

Because of the time differences between zones it is possible to have 25 hours in a day. When a steamship crosses the Atlantic Ocean in five days, it enters a new time zone every day. If it is going west it sets its clock back one hour every night. So on this ship, each day, from noon to noon, has 25 hours. When the ship travels east, it sets its clock ahead one hour every night. Then each day has only 23 hours.

Where Tuesday Becomes Wednesday

Suppose it is Tuesday noon for you by standard time. The sun is over the meridian whose local time is the standard for your zone. As the sun moves west, it carries Tuesday noon with it to zones further west. But after 24 hours it will come back to you from the east, bringing Wednesday noon. Somewhere on its journey around the earth Tuesday noon was changed to Wednesday noon. By international agreement this happens when the sun crosses the 180th

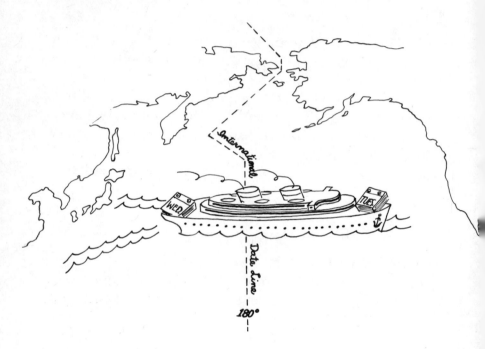

meridian, a line in the Pacific Ocean. When steamships cross this line going west, they move the calendar ahead one day. When they cross the line going east, they move the calendar back one day. Because of this, if you are on a ship traveling east and approaching the 180th meridian, you can make an appointment for yesterday and keep it!

Making The Sun Stand Still

There are modern Joshuas who *can* make the sun stand still! When the sun crosses the sky from east to west, carrying local noontime with it, it travels 15 degrees every hour. At the latitude of Chicago this takes it 778 miles west every hour. If a plane left Chicago and flew west at 778 miles per hour, it would keep up with the sun. Its local time would always be the same. It would have made the sun stand still.

Where Time Goes Backwards

The fastest speed ever reached by a plane is 2,070 miles per hour. This is even faster than the westward motion of the sun at the equator. A plane flying west at this speed anywhere in the world would get ahead of the sun. This means that the local time for the plane would go backwards.

When And Where

A clock showing local time can tell you *when* something happens; but, strangely enough, it can also tell you *where*. This is because of the connection of local time with longitude. If time changes one hour for every 15 degrees of longitude, then longitude changes 15 degrees for every hour of time difference. If your radio tells you it is 2 P.M. by Greenwich time, and the sun or stars tell you that it is 1 P.M. by your local time, then you know you must be on the meridian 15 degrees west of Greenwich. This is one of the ways in which navigators of ships and planes keep track of where they are as they move across the ocean.

73

CHAPTER VII

Rhythms of Life

The Living Clock

ALICE's father took a watch out of his waistcoat pocket. "Tut-tut," he said, "my watch has stopped."

"Never mind," said Alice. "I have my wrist watch with me." She pulled up her left sleeve to uncover her wrist. Tied to her wrist by a string was a fiddler crab, its over-sized left pincer swinging awkwardly. Alice studied the dark markings on his skin, and announced "It is half-past nine, and the tide is out."

No, you did not pick up the wrong book by mistake. This is still the book on "Time," although it sounds like *Alice in Wonderland*. And what sounds like fantasy is fact. You *can* tell time by the fiddler crab!

The fiddler crab is a living clock. It shows the time of the day by the color of its skin, which is dark by day and pale by night. The daytime darkening of its skin, which helps to protect the crab from the sunlight and from its enemies, follows a regular 24-hour rhythm. The color rhythm of the crab matches exactly the daily rhythm of the sun, the rhythm of day and night.

But is the crab really keeping time? Isn't it only responding to sunlight, growing darker when the light strikes it, and becoming pale again when daylight fades? To answer

this question, biologists who were studying the crab kept
him in a dark room for two months. They found that even
when no daylight strikes him his skin still changes color
with a regular rhythm, keeping pace with the rhythm of
day and night outside. This proved that he wasn't merely
following the rhythm of the sun, but had a built-in rhythm
of his own. The color rhythm of the crab must have developed, through millions of years of evolution, in response
to the rhythm of the sun. But by now it needs no outside
regulator. It is now regulated inside the living body of the
crab.

Two Rhythms In One

While the skin of the fiddler crab is dark all through the daytime, there is one part of the day when it is extra-dark. Biologists recorded the time when the skin is darkest. They found that each day this happens 50 minutes later than the day before. This 50-minute lag is the clue to another rhythm that the crab is following, the rhythm of the tides. In fact, the moment of greatest darkening turns out to be precisely the time of low tide on the beach where the crab was caught. The crabs follow the rhythm of the tides so closely that you can tell, by looking at a crab's skin, which beach he was taken from. In Martha's Vineyard low tide comes four hours later than at Woods Hole. Crabs from Martha's Vineyard are darkest four hours later than crabs from Woods Hole!

The Fire Of Life

The color rhythm of the fiddler crab is interesting, but not unusual among living things. There are rhythms in the movements of all living things. In fact, life itself has a rhythm, which makes every living thing a clock.

Life is like a burning flame, and the movement and rhythm of life is like the movement and rhythm of a flame.

There is movement *inside* a flame in the chemical process of burning. There is also movement outside the flame: fuel and oxygen flow into the flame, and waste products are carried away. The waste products include ashes, made up of parts of the fuel that did not burn, and smoke, made up of gases, like carbon dioxide, that are the result of burning. So, wherever there is a fire, there is an exchange of materials between the fire and its surroundings, with fuel and

76

oxygen going into the fire, and ashes and smoke coming out.

Wherever there is life there is the same kind of exchange of materials between the living body and its surroundings.

The Give And Take Of Life

All living things are made up of *cells*. The smallest living things, which can be seen only with a microscope, consist of only one cell. Large animals and plants contain millions of cells. Inside each cell there is a complicated mixture of chemicals called *protoplasm*. The life of living things is an activity of this protoplasm. There is movement inside the protoplasm in chemical actions going on all the time. These include the burning of fuels to give heat and energy of movement. But they also include processes of repair and growth. To supply the fuel and building materials needed for these processes, the living cell must get *food*. To burn the part of the food that is used as fuel, the living cell must get *oxygen*. So living things are always taking food and oxygen from their surroundings. At the same time, like a fire, they give back to their surroundings the waste products of the life process. They *excrete* the poisonous products of

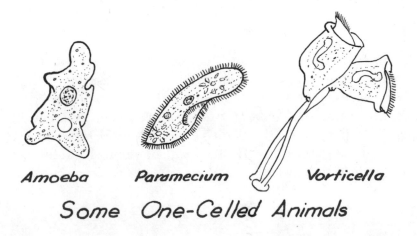

Amoeba   Paramecium   Vorticella

Some One-Celled Animals

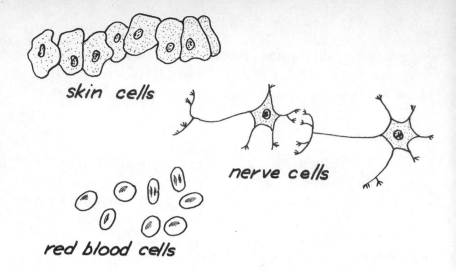

skin cells

nerve cells

red blood cells

Some Human Cells

the chemical action in the protoplasm. These may be thought of as the smoke of the life process. Animals also *eliminate* the unused parts of the food they take. These may be thought of as the ashes of the life process. The chemical process that goes on in the protoplasm of living things and that keeps the flame of life burning is called *metabolism.*

Living A Fast Life

Some animals live faster than others. This sounds like a strange statement if we think only of the passage of time. Time doesn't pass faster for one animal than for another. But the statement makes sense when we remember that life is like a flame, and the flame of life can *burn faster* in one animal than in another. In fact, some animals have to burn faster in order to live.

78

Every animal is a living radiator. The heat that is formed inside its cells is always flowing out through the animal's skin. Warm-blooded animals keep a steady temperature because the cells make a fresh supply of heat as fast as it is lost. But small animals lose heat faster than big ones, because they have more skin for every ounce of body. To make up for this greater loss of heat, the life in the cells must burn at a faster rate. That is why, among warm-blooded animals, the smaller an animal is, the faster it lives.

You can measure the speed at which an animal lives by measuring the rate at which it uses up oxygen. For example, a chicken which weighs 2,000 grams uses up 1,000 cubic centimeters of oxygen in an hour. So each gram of chicken uses up one-half cubic centimeter of oxygen in an hour. A short-tailed shrew which weighs 20 grams uses up 80 cubic centimeters of oxygen in an hour. So each gram of short-tailed shrew uses up 4 cubic centimeters of oxygen in an hour. Comparing these two animals gram for gram, we see that a short-tailed shrew uses up oxygen eight times as fast as a chicken does, so we can say it is living eight times as fast. The hummingbird, the smallest of warm-blooded animals, lives one-hundred times as fast as an elephant. Because it burns up fuel so fast, it has to have a big supply of food. That's why, when it is awake, a hummingbird is eating all the time.

Because smaller warm-blooded animals have to live faster, there is a limit to how small they can be. Animal studies show that if a warm-blooded animal were close to 2½ grams in weight, it would burn up its food so fast that it couldn't eat fast enough to keep from starving to death. So it is impossible for a mammal or bird to be as small as 2½ grams in weight.

79

When Life Slows Down

Metabolism is a two-sided process. At the same time that it breaks down and burns up part of the living protoplasm, it also refuels and repairs it. If the two sides balance, the life process goes on at an even, steady pace. But if they do not balance, metabolism goes on with a see-saw rhythm. Then there are times when the breaking down is faster than the building up. But these are followed by times when there is more building up than breaking down.

The metabolism of human beings has this see-saw rhythm. During the daytime, when we are very active, the breaking down process is so fast, that the repairing process can't keep up with it. But we make up for it at night when we go to sleep. While we sleep we burn up less fuel and give the repairing process a chance to get ahead and make up for the damage done by day. The rate of metabolism is slower while we sleep, so a man asleep lives more slowly than a man awake.

Human beings and many other animals have the habit of being awake by day and sleeping by night. Other animals, like mice, have the opposite habit. They are active by night and sleep during the day. This rhythm of waking and sleeping grew out of the rhythm of day and night, a rhythm of the sun. Through hundreds of thousands of years of evolution each animal developed the practice of being active during that part of the day when he could get the most to eat with the least risk of being eaten.

Hibernation

Winter is a difficult time for warm-blooded animals. When the air is colder, they lose their heat faster. To keep

80

up their body heat, they would have to speed up their metabolism and eat more food. But, for animals that feed on plants, winter is the time when food is scarce. Some animals get out of this tight spot by *hibernating*. They roll up into a ball, and go into a deep sleep in which their body temperature falls and their metabolism drops to a low level. They need little fuel to keep them alive while they are inactive and cooler. They live at a slow rate on the surplus food of their summer feeding, stored as fat in their bodies. When warmer weather comes, they warm up, wake up, and get to work again with a faster metabolism. The rhythm of hibernation is usually the rhythm of the seasons. It is another example of a rhythm of life that grew out of a rhythm of the sun.

Although we think of hibernation as a winter retirement from active life, there are some animals that actually hibernate once a day. The hummingbird hibernates every night. Its body temperature falls to that of the surrounding air, and its metabolism falls to one fifteenth of its daytime rate. While it is in this state, the hummingbird is scarcely able to move. Bats are also daily hibernators, but they are active at night and hibernate in the daytime.

Rhythms Of Feeding

To have fuel for its metabolism, every plant and animal must keep a flow of food into and through its body. In most cases it is not a steady flow but an interrupted flow, proceeding with its own special rhythms.

Plants get their food by making it themselves. They take water out of the ground and carbon dioxide out of the air and combine them to make the fuel foods they need to live and grow. To carry out this food-making process, they need the help of the green chlorophyll of their leaves and the energy they get from sunlight. When there is no sunlight, the food-making process stops. So the food factory in a plant follows the rhythm of the sun, working by day and stopping at night.

Animals don't have chlorophyll, so they can't make their own food. They have to get their food from plants, or from other animals. The young mammal gets his first food supply after he is born by drinking milk from his mother's breast. From the very start his feeding follows certain regular rhythms. He draws the milk from the breast by sucking. The sucking is a complicated rhythmic movement of the muscles of his mouth and throat that makes it possible for him to breathe while drinking. He drinks his fill and then sleeps. Meanwhile the milk is digested in his stomach and small intestine. When his stomach is empty, he gets hungry again, wakes up and feeds some more. So here is another rhythm, the rhythm of feeding and sleeping and feeding again. In a human baby the first feedings are every three or four hours. As he gets older, his feeding rhythm slows down until he takes on the feeding rhythm of the grownups he lives with. In the United States it is the rhythm of three meals a day.

Other grownup mammals also have a regular feeding rhythm. A hunting animal that makes a good kill will have one square meal that will satisfy him for the day. The next day he will go out hunting once more.

The Rhythm Of The Wastes

A man who tends a furnace takes care of it with a regular rhythm. As the coal burns, the ashes accumulate over the grate. At regular times during the day he shakes the ashes down to keep them from clogging the furnace and killing the fire.

The living body also has its ashes that must be removed, and a rhythm for their removal. The food that animals eat is not completely digested. In mammals the unused part of the food moves on from the small intestine to the large intestine, which serves as a reservoir for waste. From here it is expelled from the body at regular intervals. If it is not expelled in time, poisons from the wastes are absorbed into the body and injure the health of the animal. That is why it is important for people to keep their bowel movements regular.

There are other wastes in the body that result from the chemical processes in metabolism. In mammals and some other families of animals these wastes are carried by the blood from all parts of the body to the kidneys. The kidneys serve as filter stations, separating the wastes from the blood, and shipping them on to the bladder in the form of urine. The bladder is a storage tank which holds the urine until it is expelled from the body. The removal of urine from the body also follows a rhythm, usually taking place when the bladder is full.

Living Bellows

All living things need oxygen to keep the flame of life burning. One-celled animals, living in water, get the oxygen from the water that seeps into the cell through the surface of the cell. Larger animals with many cells have special organs for getting their oxygen supply.

Fishes get their oxygen through the *gills*. The oxygen passes from the water that touches the gills into the many tiny blood vessels that are there. As the water loses its

83

oxygen to the gills, it has to be moved away to make room for more water with a fresh supply of oxygen. To keep the water moving past the gills, the fish sets up a current of water, taking it in by opening and closing its mouth, and letting it out through the gill covers behind its head. The mouth and gill covers move with a regular rhythm, the rhythm of the fish's breathing.

Man and many other animals get their oxygen through the *lungs*. These are living bellows that expand and contract, taking oxygen in to pass on to the blood, and expelling carbon dioxide. The movement of air in and out of the lungs is kept up with a regular rhythm, too. Animals with a fast metabolism need a lot of oxygen, so they breathe very rapidly. Animals that live more slowly also breathe more slowly.

The amount of oxygen you need depends on how much energy you use up. When you run, or climb, or lift heavy objects, you use up a lot of energy. Then you need more oxygen, and so you breathe faster. When you sleep you use the least amount of energy, and breathe more slowly. A sleeping adult breathes about 18 times a minute.

If a person's breathing is stopped by drowning or an electric shock, his oxygen supply is cut off and he will die. But sometimes people can be saved from death by *artificial respiration*. This is a system of making their lungs expand and contract with a rhythm like the rhythm of breathing. The artificial breathing is kept up until natural breathing takes its place.

Lung Time

Any rhythm can be used for measuring time. If we wanted to, we could use the rhythm of breathing to set our clocks by, and live by lung time instead of sun time. Let's see what lung time would be like.

Suppose we use as the standard rhythm 18 breaths per minute, and measure small periods of time in "breaths." One breath would be the same as $3\frac{1}{3}$ seconds; 3 breaths would be the same as 10 seconds. A length of time that is 20 seconds by sun time would be 6 breaths by lung time.

To measure longer periods of time we could use kilo-breaths (one thousand breaths), and megabreaths (one million breaths). A kilobreath would be about 55½ minutes, or almost an hour. A megabreath would be almost 39 days long.

To change from sun time to lung time we would have to use this table:

one second = 0.3 of a breath
one minute = 18 breaths
one hour = 1,080 breaths, or 1 kilobreath and 80 breaths
one day = 25 kilobreaths and 920 breaths
one year = 9 megabreaths 466 kilobreaths and 977.8 breaths

A boy who is twelve years old by sun time would be 113 megabreaths 603 kilobreaths and 734 breaths old by lung time. His age would tell us at a glance that he had drawn 113,603,734 breaths in his lifetime.

The Living Pump

The food we eat is digested in the stomach and small intestine. That means it is changed by chemical action into a form in which it can be used by the living cells in our bodies. It is carried to the cells by the blood traveling in a network of pipes reaching all parts of the body. The blood

85

also brings to the cells the oxygen it picks up at the lungs, and removes from the cells the waste products of the life-process. These include carbon dioxide that is brought to the lungs to be breathed out, and other wastes that are removed from the blood at the kidney filter stations. The blood is kept circulating by the action of a living pump, the heart. The regular beating of the heart is another rhythm of life that marks the passage of time.

The rhythm of an animal's heartbeat depends on how fast the animal lives. The tiny heart of the fast-living hummingbird beats about 1,000 times a minute. The heart of a mouse beats about 300 times a minute. The heart of a man beats from 68 to 72 times a minute. An elephant's heartbeat is 35 to 40 times a minute.

When you run, or climb, or do hard work, you burn up more than the usual amount of fuel, and so you live faster, too. Your heart pumps faster then, to rush to your cells the extra oxygen supplied by your faster breathing.

Whaling For Science

In 1952 a man from Boston went on a whale hunt, but he was not a sailor, and he was not interested in whale oil. He was a heart specialist, and he wanted to measure the heartbeat of a whale. His expedition harpooned a whale in Bristol Bay, off the coast of Alaska. The harpoon he used was one of special design, connected by a cable to an electrocardiograph that made a record of the whale's heartbeat. The whale's heartbeat was 20 times a minute.

The Artificial Heart

If the cells of the human brain get no oxygen for two minutes, they die. That's why a person dies if his heart stops

beating and the blood no longer brings oxygen to his brain.
One of the big problems of surgery has been to find a way
of operating on a heart without interrupting the flow of
blood. The problem was recently solved by the invention
of an artificial heart that imitates the heartbeat and does
the work of the heart while the heart is freed for repairs.

The Amoeba's Water Pump

Even the smallest of animals have regular rhythms. A
good example is the "water pump" of the amoeba and other
one-celled animals.

The amoeba is a tiny blob of protoplasm too small to be
seen without a microscope. It lives in water, so that water
is seeping into its body all the time. Excess water is removed by the rhythmic pumping of a "contractile vacuole."

87

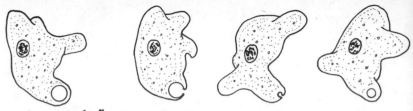

Amoeba's "water pump"- the contractile vacuole

This is a little bubble in the protoplasm where the excess water collects, until the bubble contracts and expels the water out of the body of the amoeba. The regular growing and contracting of the vacuole is like the pumping of a ship's pump, and serves the same purpose—it keeps the amoeba from being flooded by water.

Rhythms Of Growth

Animals and plants grow, and the movement of growth also has its rhythm. Each large plant or animal is made up of many cells. Part of the food used by each cell is built into the body of the cell, so that the cell grows. But a growing cell doesn't grow larger forever. After it reaches a certain size, it divides into two small cells just like itself. Then each new cell grows until it also divides. Growing follows dividing, and dividing follows growing. Through this rhythm in a growing plant or animal the number of its cells is increased at the same time that it grows in size.

How a cell divides

Tree Ring Time

The growth of most trees is regulated by the rhythm of the seasons. In the springtime the sap begins to flow, carrying food from the soil to the living cells. Sunlight, captured by the leaves, helps the tree make more food out of water and carbon dioxide. This food is built into the growing cells, and the tree becomes taller and wider. In the fall, when the sunlight is weaker, and chill winds blow, the leaves wither and fall, and growth stops. During the winter the tree is asleep, waiting to be wakened by the warmth of the sun's rays the following spring.

The living cells in a tree trunk are just under the bark. Each year, when these cells grow, they build a ring of

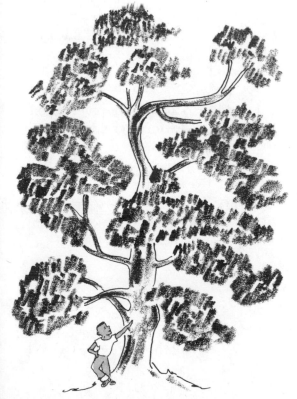

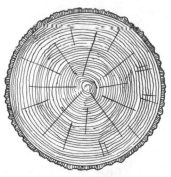

You can find out how old a tree is by counting its rings.

wood around the older part of the tree inside. If you cut through the trunk of a tree you can see these rings. By counting them you can find out how many years the tree has been alive. On the west slope of the Sierra Nevada Mountains in California there are giant sequoia trees, some of them 275 feet high and 25 feet wide. The rings in these trees show that they are thousands of years old. The oldest of those still standing is probably between 3,000 and 4,000 years old.

The Rhythm Of The Chain Of Life

All living things grow old and die. But life continues, because living things reproduce—they have children like themselves. In this way a chain of life is formed. Each living thing is a link in this chain, connecting his ancestors with his offspring, linking the past with the future. The growth of this chain goes on with a regular rhythm as link is added to link.

One of these rhythms is the rhythm of the generations. Young people grow up, marry, and have children. Then their own children, the new generation, go through the same cycle. If, on the average, young people have their first children when they are twenty-five years old, then each generation exists twenty-five years before producing the next. Every twenty-five years a new generation appears, and four generations span a century of time.

The Rhythm Of The Butterfly

In insect life the rhythm of the generations is combined with another rhythm, the rhythm of *metamorphosis,* or change from one stage of life to another. You can watch

90

this fascinating rhythm in your own room by raising butterflies in a jar. Here are directions for doing it.

In June and July watch for the appearance of the Monarch butterfly, a beautiful creature with bright black, brown, and white markings. When you know that they are in your neighborhood, start hunting for Monarch eggs. Find a place where the common milkweed grows, and examine its leaves. If you are patient and careful you will find on some leavs a tiny, white, dome-shaped object about the size of a pinhead. This is the egg of the Monarch butterfly. Gently remove this leaf and place it in a glass jar. Before you cover the jar, punch air holes in the cover.

The Monarch egg hatches three days after it was laid. A tiny striped caterpillar eats its way out of the egg case and immediately begins eating the milkweed leaf. Soon its bright yellow, black, and white stripes will be visible. It eats almost all the time, and grows rapidly for about two weeks. During this time you will have to keep it supplied with fresh milkweed leaves, and you should clean out the jar from time to time. When the caterpillar is fully grown (about two inches long) it will weave a mat at the top of the jar, hook its tail into it, and then hang head down. During the next few hours, the caterpillar will squirm violently. Its skin will split and peel off, and the caterpillar will contract to become a chrysalis. The chrysalis looks like a jade-colored bead studded with golden nails. In this stage it will be absolutely motionless for about ten days. Meanwhile, great changes are taking place inside. At the end of the ten-day period the chrysalis will become darker, and you'll see the markings of a butterfly's wings inside. If you watch it closely now, you may catch the time when the butterfly comes out. The chrysalis splits open at the bottom, and the butterfly slowly swings

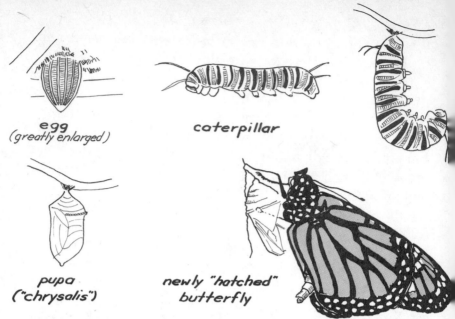

egg
(greatly enlarged)

caterpillar

pupa
("chrysalis")

newly "hatched"
butterfly

LIFE CYCLE OF THE MONARCH BUTTERFLY

out, holding on with its legs. Its wings are tiny at first, but immediately begin to grow as the butterfly pumps fluid from its abdomen into the veins of the wings. The wings grow longer, like crepe paper being stretched, until they are full size. In a few hours, after the wings have dried, the butterfly will be able to fly. Release it, and it will fly from flower to flower, sucking nectar from the blossoms with its long coiled tongue. After it mates, the female butterfly will lay eggs on the milkweed plant, and the cycle will start all over again, from egg to caterpillar to chrysalis to butterfly, following a regular rhythm.

The Rhythm Of The Fruit

Some plants live for only one year, and produce seeds from which new plants will grow the next year. Other

92

plants live for many years, but grow a new crop of seed-bearing fruit each year. This adds another rhythm to the rhythm of reproduction, the rhythm of the fruit. It is part of the annual rhythm of growth of the plant, and usually follows the rhythm of the seasons. The farmer who cultivates these plants studies their rhythms and uses them to regulate his work. He learns the proper time for planting and cultivating, spraying, pruning and harvesting, in order to get the most seed or fruit of the best quality.

The connection of the rhythm of the fruit with the rhythm of the seasons was noticed thousands of years ago by the earliest farmers. Because of this connection they knew they should study the changes in the seasons. That's why the calendar was among the important inventions of every ancient people.

Children Of The High Tide

The tide flows in and out at the seashore every 12½ hours. But every fifteen days, when the moon's pull on the ocean is re-enforced by the pull of the sun, there is an extra-high tide that reaches further than usual up on the beach. On the nights of this highest tide, the grunion, small fish that live near shore in the Pacific Ocean, swim in very close. The waves toss them onto the beach, where they deposit their eggs and sperm before jumping back into the water. The fertilized eggs develop in the wet sand for fifteen days. Then, when the next extra-high tide comes in, the water level reaches the young fish, and they swim out to sea. This is one of many interesting cases in which the rhythm of reproduction of animals is regulated by the rhythm of the tides.

93

CHAPTER VIII

Rhythm in the Rocks

Water Cuts Rock

WATER is soft, and rock is hard. In spite of that, water can and does cut through rock. One of the great natural wonders of the world is the Grand Canyon of the Colorado River. It is over 200 miles long, 1 mile deep, and about 10 miles wide. The sides of the canyon are great cliffs of solid rock forming a series of steps, each hundreds of feet high. This giant ditch is the work of the Colorado River, which has cut through the solid rock to reach its present channel at the bottom of the canyon.

The Mighty Raindrop

Catch some raindrops on your palm. See how gently they trickle down your skin. But the same power that makes them flow gently on your palm gives them the strength to cut through rocks. When rainwater collects on the ground, some of it sinks into the earth. The rest immediately begins to flow downhill. This is the beginning of a long journey that takes it from brooks to rivers, and from rivers down to the sea. As rainwater flows along the ground, it picks up soil and sand and carries it along. Where the flow is fast and strong it can pick up pebbles, too. A rapidly flowing brook can carry stones, and a

94

swiftly flowing river can move boulders. With the sand and stone that it carries, flowing water can grind its way into rock. In this way water keeps wearing down the ground over which it flows. The flow of water is strongest in the springtime, when winter snows melt, and in the fall, when rains are heavy. It is weakest in the cold winter and the dry summer. So the grinding action of water turns the rhythm of the seasons into a rhythm of the wearing down of rocks.

The mud and rock carried off by streams adds up to vast amounts. Each year the Mississippi River carries 730,000,000 tons of solid matter into the Gulf of Mexico. By carrying off such big chunks of land each year, the rivers of the United States are steadily reducing its average height above sea level. They are wearing down the land at the rate of 1 foot in 9,000 years. If this rate were to continue, the United States would be worn down to sea level in about 23 million years.

River Time

When a river cuts through rock, its grinding action can serve as a rough measure of time. At Niagara Falls, the torrents of falling water keep wearing away the rock of the Falls. As a result, the Falls are retreating upstream at the rate of 3 feet a year. At this rate, it must have taken the Falls about 12,000 years to travel to their present position from Lewiston seven miles away.

The rate at which the Colorado River is cutting through rock can be judged by the amount of mud and stone it carries. From information of this kind geologists figure that it took the river several million years to carve out the Grand Canyon.

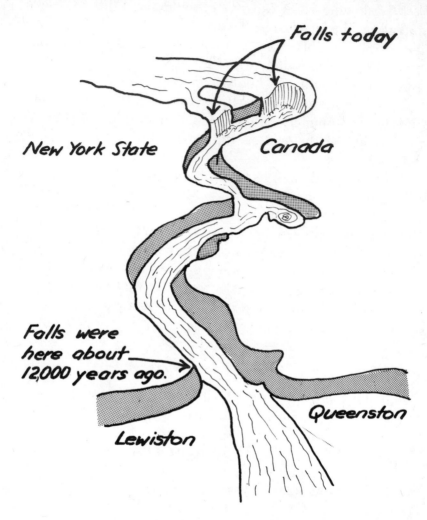

Falls today

New York State

Canada

Falls were here about 12,000 years ago.

Lewiston

Queenston

How Niagara Falls
Moved Seven Miles

Dropping The Load

When streams flow down a steep slope, they flow quickly, and pick up a lot of mud and stone. But when they reach more level land, they slow down. Some of the mud and stone falls to the bottom, where it piles up year after year. So, while streams wear down the land in high places, they build it up in low places. The result is a steady leveling of the land through which the streams flow.

The streams drop the rest of their load when they reach the end of their journey in a lake or in the sea. Here, too, the bottom is built up, layer on layer, year after year. This building-up process is another rhythm of the rocks.

The Last Ice Age

There was a time when large parts of North America and Europe were covered by glaciers, which are big thick sheets of ice. When the ice melted, many lakes where formed. Streams of ice water flowed into the lakes, where the mud they carried settled to the bottom. Year after year this mud piled up, forming thick deposits of clay. In the springtime, when the streams were most active, the coarser particles of mud settled. In the wintertime, when the water was calm, the smallest particles settled over them. So the clay was laid down in distinct double sheets of fine clay over coarse clay.

Some of these lakes were completely filled up, and, after the ice sheets were gone, they dried out. Where the old lake beds have been cut open, the separate sheets of clay can easily be seen, even though they are only a fraction of an inch thick. What's more, they can be counted. Since each double band of fine over coarse clay was laid

97

down in one year, counting the layers serves to measure the time it took to fill up the lake. From counts of this kind, geologists have figured out that the last Ice Age ended about 10,000 years ago.

The Rhythm Of The Ages

The action of flowing water is wearing the continents down. If this action were unopposed, the continents would have disappeared a long time ago. But when, over millions of years, large masses of earth are carried by the rivers from one place to another, this upsets the balance in the earth's crust. For this and other reasons, the earth's crust buckles, masses of land are raised high above sea level, and mountains are built. Once the land is raised, streams flow more rapidly, and the wearing down process starts all over again. So the history of the continents is a see-saw history of raising up and wearing down, in one gigantic rhythm of the ages.

The Grand Canyon Layer Cake

When river mud settles at the bottom of the sea, it is packed hard as more mud piles up on top of it. In this way rocks like shale and sandstone are formed under water. Later, when the earth's crust buckles, these under-water rocks may be raised up out of the sea. Large areas of the continents are made up of these layered rocks, showing that they were once under water. One of these natural "layer cakes" of rock is the plateau through which the Colorado River flows. The river has cut through the layers like a knife, exposing them to view in the Grand Canyon.

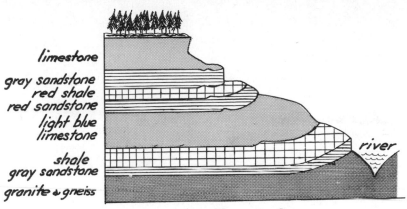

limestone
gray sandstone
red shale
red sandstone
light blue
limestone
shale
gray sandstone
granite & gneiss

river

Rock Layers at Grand Canyon

The layers of rock in the Grand Canyon are of different colors, from white and buff to bright red and dull green. At the bottom of the cliffs the river is cutting through granite and gneiss, the original rocks on top of which the first layers were formed. Above the granite are the layers in this order: gray sandstone, shale, limestone, red sandstone, red shale, gray sandstone, and limestone again. The arrangement of the layers is a clue to their age. The oldest rocks are at the bottom, the youngest ones at the top. The study of rock layers like this one, all over the world, was the first step toward discovering the timetable of the earth's history.

Life In The Rocks

When a region like the Arizona plateau is raised up out of the sea, rainwater gets to work and starts wearing it down. In some places, whole layers of rock have been completely removed by the water. So the arrangement of rocks in layers is not a perfect guide to their age. But there

99

is another clue inside the rocks themselves. Many of the rocks contain fossils, the remains of plants or animals that lived at the time the rocks were formed. These animals and plants are the ancestors and distant relatives of all the animals and plants alive today. Different animals and plants lived in different ages, and scientists can tell which ones came first. The study of fossils and their family tree was the second step toward discovering the timetable of the earth's history.

Shell Fossils in Rock

The Salt Clock

The study of layered rocks and fossils tells scientists which of two rocks is older. But it doesn't tell *how old* they are. So geologists began searching for ways of measuring the age as well as the arrangement of past happenings on the earth. The Irish scientist Joly found a clue in the salt of the sea. He argued that the salt in the sea was brought there by the rivers, which keep washing it out of the rocks. By measuring how much salt the rivers bring to the sea each year, he thought he could figure out how many years it took to make the sea as salty as it is now. His calculation showed that the oceans must be at least 100 million years old. Joly's salt clock was not a very good one, though, because the rivers don't always carry the same amount of salt each year. In fact, many times in the past, the continents were low or mostly under water. At those times the flow of salt into the sea was much slower than it is now.

The Earth's Timetable

A real timetable of the earth's history became possible when scientists found a reliable clock for measuring the age of rocks. This is the uranium clock, and others like it, described in the next chapter. Here is the timetable that has been discovered with their help:

4½	billion years ago:	Beginning of the earth
2	billion years ago:	Formation of the oldest rocks known; beginning of life
600	million years ago:	Beginning of the age of animals without backbones
400	million years ago:	Beginning of the age of fishes
350	million years ago:	Beginning of the age of amphibians; formation of large coal beds
230	million years ago:	Beginning of the age of reptiles, when dinosaurs roamed the world
100	million years ago:	Beginning of the age of mammals
1	million years ago:	Beginning of the ice age and the age of man

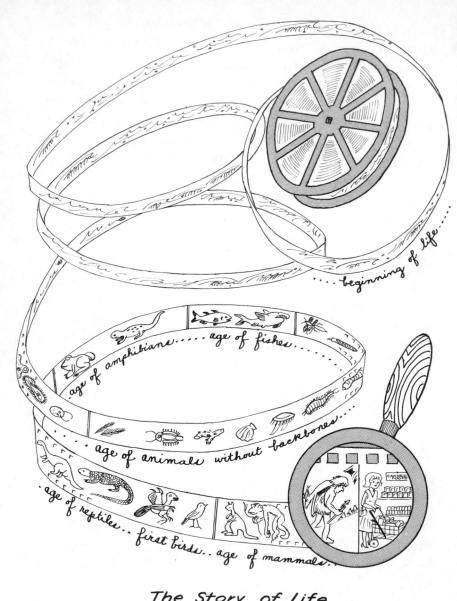

age of amphibians..... age of fishes.....

beginning of life.....

age of animals without backbones....

age of reptiles.. first birds.. age of mammals..

The Story of Life

CHAPTER IX

Rhythm in the Atom

Nature's Building Blocks

WE have found rhythm in the sky and rhythm in the rocks; rhythm in life, and rhythm in lifeless things. So we won't be surprised to find that there is also rhythm in the atoms, the building blocks of nature.

All things are made up of atoms. There are about a hundred different kinds of atoms, ranging from hydrogen which is the lightest, and is found everywhere in space, to the heaviest ones, like plutonium, which are found only where man makes them. All of the atoms are so tiny that they cannot be seen even with the most powerful microscope.

Messages From The Atom

Although we cannot see separate atoms, scientists have learned many facts about them because the atoms send us messages. Solids, liquids, and gases sometimes glow or send out light. Some of this light is a message from inside the atom. The light that comes from a neon lamp is a message from the atoms of neon gas inside the lamp. The sunlight that we get every day is a message from the atoms in the glowing gases of the sun.

The messages are in code, and their parts are all jumbled together. The first step in decoding the messages is to separate the parts. This can be done by passing the light through a glass prism. If you do this with ordinary sunlight you find that it is really a mixture of many colors. The prism separates the colors, spreading them out in a band of colors called the *spectrum*. Each color, from red to violet, is part of the message from the atoms in the sun.

The *rainbow* is a spectrum you sometimes see immediately after a rain. It is formed when the water droplets in the air do the work of a prism, separating the colors in the sunlight. The beveled edge of the mirror in your bathroom also works like a prism, separating the colors in the sunlight that strikes it. That is why you sometimes see a spectrum reflected from the mirror onto your bathroom wall.

The Rhythms Of Color

Scientists studying light have found that it is a kind of vibration or rhythm, and each color has a rhythm of its own. They call the vibration a wave motion because it travels in space the way a wave travels on the surface of water. When waves travel across water, the water keeps

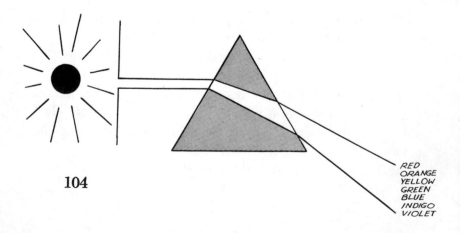

104

RED
ORANGE
YELLOW
GREEN
BLUE
INDIGO
VIOLET

bobbing up and down. The number of times the water bobs up and down in one second, the rhythm of the wave, is called its *frequency*. Light waves also have a frequency. The rhythm or frequency of green light, for example, is 600 million million times a second. The rhythms of light give us clues to the rhythms inside the atoms which send out the light.

Fingerprinting The Atom

If a gas that has atoms of only one kind is made to glow, it does not send out all colors, but only certain special colors. When these colors are spread out in a spectrum, they form a series of disconnected colored lines. Each line is a different color, with a different rhythm.

The colors you get from one kind of atom are different from the colors you get from another kind of atom. For example, if you sprinkle some table salt over a gas flame, the flame will turn yellow. The yellow glow comes from the sodium atoms in the salt. But the glow of a neon lamp is red. The red comes from the neon atoms inside the lamp. Because each different kind of atom sends out its own special set of colors, you can identify an atom by the lines in its spectrum, the way you identify a person by the lines in his fingerprints.

Atoms can absorb light, as well as send it out. If light of all colors is passed through a gas, the atoms of the gas will remove some of the light. The colors the atoms re-

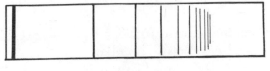

The Hydrogen Spectrum

move are the same colors they normally send out. If the light mixture is then spread out to form a spectrum, there will be dark lines in the places of the missing colors. These dark lines, too, are like fingerprints of the atoms, and serve to identify them.

The Dance Of The Electrons

When an atom sends out light the rhythm of the light comes from the rhythm in the atom. By studying the light, physicists have been able to form pictures of the atom, with its rhythms. They have learned that each atom consists of a nucleus surrounded by a cloud of one or more electrons. The electrons are in a perpetual dance, with definite but complicated rhythms. The outer structure of the atom is the structure of these rhythms of the electrons.

Splitting The Atom

Every atom has an inner structure, too, the structure of its nucleus. The nucleus is made up of protons and neutrons locked together in a dance of their own. To study a nucleus, a physicist smashes it open by hitting it with another particle. Splitting atoms in this way has given us information about the rhythms inside the nucleus. It has also given us a way of releasing the great amounts of energy that are locked up inside the nucleus.

Atoms That Split Themselves

Some atoms don't have to be split by us. They split by themselves without being bombarded from the outside. Every once in a while one of these atoms fires a piece out

106

of its nucleus, and by changing its inside structure it changes itself into another kind of atom. Atoms that break up in this way, without any outside help, are called *radio-active*. The first atom found to be radioactive was uranium. Physicists have since found in nature other radioactive atoms, like radium and thorium, and have made many more, like neptunium, that aren't found in nature at all.

The Uranium Clock

In a sample of uranium, the atoms don't all split at the same time. They split one after the other with a definite rhythm, or at a definite rate. The steady rhythm of the splitting of uranium can be used as a clock for measuring the age of the rocks in which the uranium is found.

When a uranium atom splits, it breaks up several times, becoming something else each time it loses a piece of it-self, until finally it ends up as an atom of lead. As time passes and more atoms in a lump of uranium break up, the lump has less and less uranium and more and more lead in it. So, by measuring the amount of lead in a sample of uranium, scientists can figure out how old the uranium is.

Uranium breaks up, or *decays*, very slowly. Scientists measure the speed of decay by finding the *half-life*, the amount of time it takes for half of the atoms in a sample to decay. The half-life of uranium is 7,600 million years. For this reason the uranium clock has been useful for measuring very long periods of time. By measuring the amount of lead and uranium in a rock sample taken from the Black Hills of South Dakota, scientists found that it is 1.6 billion years old. It is the oldest known mineral in the United States.

The Age Of The Earth

The uranium clock has been used to measure the age of the earth.

According to recent theories of the formation of the earth, the earth grew up by the coming together of particles of dust and rock flying through space. In fact, the earth is still growing in this way, because more rocks keep crashing onto the earth from the surrounding space each day. These rocks are called *meteors*. As they speed into the earth's atmosphere and rub against the air, the friction makes them hot. Most of them burn up with a flash of light. These are the "shooting stars" that you can see streaking across the sky on any clear night. Occasionally a big one doesn't burn out completely, and reaches the ground. One that reaches the ground is called a *meteorite*. If we assume that all the particles that came together to make the earth were formed at about the same time in space, then we can measure the age of the earth by measuring the age of a meteorite. In 1954, some physicists, by measuring the amount of lead in a meteorite, found that the earth is about 4.5 billion years old.

The Carbon Clock

One of the radioactive elements recently discovered is a carbon atom called Carbon 14. Most carbon atoms have 12 particles in the nucleus, 6 protons and 6 neutrons. But Carbon 14 has fourteen particles in the nucleus, 6 protons and 8 neutrons. Carbon 14 is being made all the time in the upper air surrounding the earth. Cosmic rays, which are fast-moving nuclei that crash into the air from outer space, sometimes smash an atom and release some neu-

108

trons. When a neutron hits a nitrogen atom, the nitrogen throws out a charged particle and turns into Carbon 14. Out of every thousand million carbon atoms in the air, only one of them is Carbon 14. But this is still enough to make it possible to detect it with a Geiger counter. Carbon 14 has a half-life of 5,568 years. If the Carbon 14 in a sample of air is allowed to decay without being replaced, then after five half-lives, or about 28,000 years, only one thirty-second of the Carbon 14 will be left. Detection of even this small amount is now possible. So the carbon clock can be used to measure lengths of time up to about 28,000 years, by measuring how much Carbon 14 has decayed.

The Age Of Dead Plants

The Carbon 14 in the air is decaying all the time. But it is also being replaced all the time by new Carbon 14 atoms formed from nitrogen, because there is a steady stream of cosmic rays raining in on the earth. As a result, in any sample of air, the part of its carbon that is made up of Carbon 14 is always the same.

Plants get their carbon by breathing in carbon dioxide from the air. Because the living cells of plants keep getting fresh carbon from the air, they are also getting with it a fresh supply of Carbon 14. But as soon as the cells die, they no longer get fresh Carbon 14 to replace the atoms that decay. So the amount of Carbon 14 begins to decrease. That is why, after a plant dies, the amount of Carbon 14 in it can tell you how long it is since it died.

Checking The Clock

When scientists got the idea of measuring time in this way, they tried it first on a few things whose ages they already knew, to be sure that the method really works. They measured the amount of Carbon 14 in the oldest part of a sequoia tree, the dead heartwood at the center. Then their calculations showed that the tree must be about 3,000 years old. The number of rings in the tree proved that this was correct.

They tried the method, too, on old wood and mummy cases 4,600 years old, taken from ancient tombs in Egypt. In each case the age found by the carbon clock turned out to be correct.

The Age Of Dead Animals

When archeologists dig up old ruins, they sometimes find the bones of animals people had eaten long ago. By measuring the amount of Carbon 14 in the bones, they can find out how old they are, because the carbon clock works for dead animals, too. Animals get their carbon by eating plants or other animals. So they also have a fresh supply of Carbon 14 as long as they live. But as soon as they die, the carbon clock begins to work. The Carbon 14 in them that decays is not replaced, and the age of any bones or other remains that are preserved can be measured by the amount of Carbon 14 that is left.

The End Of The Ice Age

By counting the layers of clay in old glacial lake bottoms, geologists have found that the ice age ended 10,000 years ago. Tree pollen found at the bottom of the lake mud can also be used to find out how far back in time the ice age was. The Carbon 14 in the pollen confirms the fact that the last ice age ended about 10,000 years ago.

Camp sites of ancient tribes of men who lived in the ice age have been dug out of the ground. Bits of charcoal or burnt animal bone have been found at these camp sites. The carbon clock has been used to see how old they are, and the result agrees with the age shown by the pollen and the layers of clay.

How Old Is Wine?

The label on a wine bottle tells you how old it is. But if you don't believe the label, you can call in a physicist to measure the age of the wine for you. He will use a Geiger counter to measure the amount of tritium, or heavy hydrogen, in the wine. That will tell you its age, because tritium, too, is radioactive and can be used as an atomic clock.

Tritium is a variety of heavy hydrogen formed by cosmic ray collisions with atoms in the air. It is carried down to the ground in rain water all the time. Growing grape vines and all other plants draw the water in through their roots, so, as they grow, they have a fresh supply of tritium to replace those atoms that are decaying. But once the grapes are picked, this supply of tritium is cut off, and the amount of tritium in the grapes begins to decrease. It continues to decrease, too, in the grape juice and wine made from the grapes. The half-life of tritium is 12½ years. Measuring the amount of tritium can be used for measuring ages up to 30 years.

111

CHAPTER X

Rhythms in Space

Our Whirling Universe

THE daily motion of the sun and stars across the sky is really a rhythm of the earth. It is the earth's rotation that makes them seem to move around us. But there are other rhythms in the sky that come from motions out in space. Galileo discovered a real rhythm of the sun when he looked at it through his first telescope. He saw dark spots on the sun, and found that they move steadily across it. This showed that the sun is spinning on an axis the way the earth does. The sun makes a full turn in about 25 days. Now we know that spinning is a common thing in space. Our closest neighbors, the sun, the moon, and the planets, all spin. And the farthest objects we can see with modern telescopes, the giant families of stars called spiral nebulae, are spinning, too. We live in a whirling universe of spinning stars and families of stars.

The Sunspot Cycle

The sunspots Galileo saw have a rhythm of their own. They are magnetic storms on the surface of the sun, and are born, develop, and die. Most of the time they are scarce, but every eleven years they are numerous.

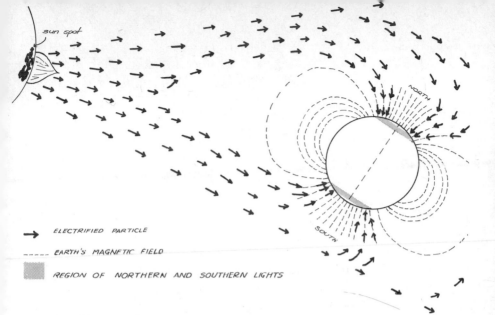

ELECTRIFIED PARTICLE
EARTH'S MAGNETIC FIELD
REGION OF NORTHERN AND SOUTHERN LIGHTS

The eleven-year rhythm of the sunspots has an important effect here on the earth. The sunspots shoot out large streams of electrified particles. Some of them, after traveling the distance of 93 million miles from the sun, enter the earth's atmosphere. Because of the earth's magnetism, they stream in near its north and south magnetic poles. Their collisions with the upper air cause flashes of light seen at night as the Northern Lights and Southern Lights. They also make electrical storms that interfere with radio reception. In a year when sunspot activity is very high, the weather is warmer, trees grow extra-thick rings, and the glaciers on high mountains begin to melt.

Stars That Throb

Most stars shine with a steady light. But some stars are blinking all the time. They change their brightness with a regular rhythm, growing dim, and bright, and dim again. This was first noticed in a star in the faint constellation

Cepheus, near *Cassiopeia.* So now all stars that blink in the same way are called *Cepheids.* The blinking is caused by a throbbing of the star, expanding and contracting with a regular rhythm.

Astronomers found that the rhythms of the Cepheids depend on how bright they are. Those with a slow rhythm are bright stars. Those with a rapid rhythm are faint stars. This fact makes it possible to use the Cepheids as a *yardstick of the sky.* If a cluster of stars has Cepheids in it, their rhythm is a clue to how bright they are. But the farther away the cluster is, the fainter the stars will look. So, by comparing how bright they really are with how bright they look to us, the astronomers can figure out how far away they are. In this way they use the rhythms of the Cepheids to measure distances in space.

Telltale Rhythms

Starlight, like sunlight, is a mixture of colors that can be separated by a prism. Each color has a rhythm of its own. By studying the rhythms in starlight, astronomers have learned many things about the stars.

When the colors in the light of a star are separated to form a spectrum, many dark lines are seen where some of the colors are missing. These dark lines are caused by the atoms near the surface of the star, which absorb some of the colors as the light passes, on its way out. It's as though each atom put its fingerprint on the light as a message to us on the earth. These dark-line messages tell us what the stars are made of. They show that the atoms in the stars are the same as the atoms in the sun and on the earth.

Some of the stars are moving away from us. As they send

114

us wave after wave of light, each later wave starts its journey to us from a greater distance. This delays the waves and slows down the rhythm of the light. As a result, all the dark lines in the spectrum are shifted toward the red end. By measuring this change in rhythm, astronomers figure out how fast the star is moving away from us. When a star is moving toward us, the rhythms of the colors are speeded up, and the dark lines are shifted to the violet end of the spectrum.

The colors in light from distant spiral nebulae all show a shift toward the red. This shows that these nebulae are moving away from us. Curiously, the farther away they are, the faster they move. The fastest nebulae that have been observed are retreating at 86,000 miles a second, about one-half of the speed of light.

Radio Messages From Space

Light waves have a very fast rhythm. Green light, for example, has a rhythm of 600 million million vibrations a

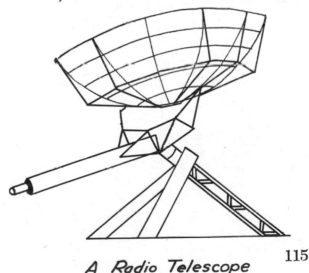

A Radio Telescope

115

second. Recently, astronomers discovered that some stars are sending out radio waves, too. These waves have a slower rhythm than light, and can be detected with special "radio telescopes."

There are parts of the sky that have dark patches. These are caused by dust clouds in space which keep the light of the stars behind them from coming through. But the dust doesn't stop radio waves. So astronomers can now "see" through the dust clouds with their new radio telescopes.

A large part of the dust in space is made up of hydrogen molecules. It has been found that these molecules also send out radio waves, with a rhythm of 1,420 million vibrations a second. By studying these hydrogen radio signals, astronomers have gathered many facts about the positions, shapes, and movements of the dust clouds. They have proved from these facts that the Milky Way, the star family to which our sun belongs, has a pinwheel shape like the spiral nebulae of outer space.

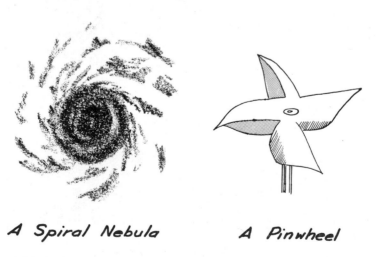

A Spiral Nebula   A Pinwheel

CHAPTER XI

Rhythms in Work and Play

WE spend a good part of our time working to make things we use, and much of the rest of our time enjoying nature and the things we make. Because there are rhythms everywhere, it is not surprising that our work and play are often built around these rhythms.

We Dance And We Sing

In every part of the world people dance. They walk, run, or glide, circle, hop, and whirl, or bounce and kick. Their dance may be a fox trot, waltz, or polka, a tango, rhumba, or mambo. It may be an American Square Dance, a Russian Troika, a Swedish Varsovienne, or an Italian Tarantella. But, in all cases, the movements have a rhythm.

And when they dance, there is music. The Spaniard may play a guitar, the Italian an accordion, the American a banjo, and the Persian a flute. But all will sing.

The Rhythms Of Music

There is music for every mood. There is slow music that is sad, and snappy music for dancing. There are strong rhythms for marching, and lilting melodies for singing. There are modest ballads, as simple as the peasant huts in which they were born. And there are towering

117

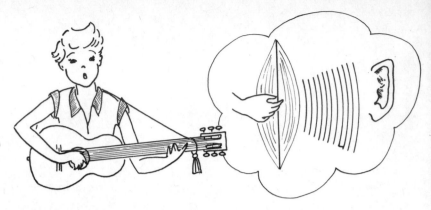

symphonies as complex and as carefully built as a great cathedral. In all of them there are rhythms within rhythms within rhythms. First, there is the rhythm of the theme or melody. In a ballad, it is the rhythm of the rhyming lines. Then, within each line there is the rhythm of the measure, like the *one*-two-three, *one*-two-three beat of a waltz. Finally, each chord or note itself is a rhythm.

The Sounds We Hear

A musical tone is a vibration, usually carried to our ears by the air. If a wheel with holes in it is turned past a stream of compressed air, each time the stream blows through another hole, it will give the surrounding air a push. If the wheel turns slowly, so that the stream blows through less than twenty holes in a second, our ears de-

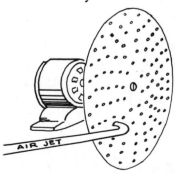

AIR JET

118

tect each push as a separate pulse. But when the wheel turns faster, so that there are twenty or more pulses a second, what we hear is a musical tone. The faster the frequency or rhythm of the pulses, the higher is the pitch of the tone we hear. But if the frequency goes above 20,000 cycles (20,000 pulses per second), we don't hear any sound at all, because our ears don't respond to rhythms that are that fast.

Families Of Tones

Musical tones are used in families. Melodies are built by choosing notes from a *scale,* a family of tones arranged in order of frequency. A piano scale that uses all black and white keys has 13 notes, and the frequency of the last one is double the frequency of the first one. The gap between the begi...ing and the end of the scale is called an *octave.* "A" above middle "C" has a frequency of 440 cycles. The "A" an octave higher is 880 cycles. The notes between them mark equal steps, called half-tone intervals, in the climb from the lower frequency to the higher one. To go up a half-tone interval from any note, you multiply the frequency by 1.059. This strange number is used because, when you multiply a frequency by this number twelve times, you end up with double the frequency,

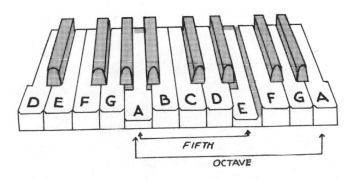

so that twelve half-tone steps carry you up an octave.

When notes are played together, they are chosen to make pleasing sounds called *chords*. The most important chord, called a "fifth," is the one in which the higher note has one and a half times as many vibrations per second as the lower one.

Natural Rhythms

Every pendulum has its own natural rhythm. The rhythm with which it swings depends on its length. Objects that make sounds when they vibrate have their natural rhythms too. The rhythm of a string that is plucked depends on its length, its weight, and how tightly it is stretched. The rhythm of a wind instrument like a clarinet depends on the length of the column of air that vibrates in it. This is controlled by opening and closing holes in the instrument. You can make a simple wind instrument out of pop bottles filled with different amounts of water. Because the air columns in them have different lengths, each will make a different musical tone when you blow into it.

Anything that vibrates when struck has its own musical rhythm. Strike a table fork on the edge of your kitchen table. As it vibrates it will sing in a special tone, always the same. Strike the edge of a tumbler with your finger. It, too, will sing, as it vibrates with its natural rhythm.

You can make a string vibrate without plucking it. All you have to do is sing to it. Sing a tone of the scale into a piano while you step on the loud pedal. The piano will sing the tone back to you. This happens because the natural rhythm of one of the strings is the same as the rhythm of the tone. Because the vibrations of the air match

the rhythm of the string, they start the string vibrating and then you can hear it.

In the same way, you can use music to break a glass. If you play the tone that has the natural rhythm of the glass, the glass will begin to vibrate. If the tone is loud enough, the glass will vibrate violently and shatter.

Sounds We Don't Hear

Vibrations with a rhythm that is higher than 20,000 cycles are called *ultra-sonic*, because we cannot hear them. The cry of a bat is ultra-sonic, having a frequency of 48,000 cycles. But the bat's ears are better than ours. He can hear up to 60,000 cycles. This makes it possible for him to "hear" his way in the dark. As he flies around at night, he makes his ultra-sonic call. If it is reflected back to him, he knows there is an obstacle in front of him, and he turns aside.

Recently a washing machine was invented that uses ultra-sonic vibrations. In this machine the water vibrates so fast that it shakes the dirt right out of the clothes.

121

Imitating The Atoms

To get rhythms that are much faster than ultra-sonic vibrations, we had to imitate the atoms. This was done when radio was invented, because radio waves are vibrations like the light waves sent out by vibrating atoms.

Radio waves are broadcast into space when an electric current goes back and forth very quickly in the *oscillator* of a transmitter. The rhythm of the oscillator is based on the team work of two parts, the *capacitor* and the *coil*. The capacitor is like a storage tank for holding electrical power. In its simplest form it consists of two plates facing each other. When the capacitor is charged, electrons are removed from one plate, and piled up on the other, so that one plate has too few, and the other has too many. When the capacitor is connected to the coil, the electrons have a path they can follow, so they start flowing from where they are crowded, streaming back to the other plate. But the coil behaves in a funny way. It doesn't like currents to change as they pass through it. So when a current tries to speed up, the coil slows it down. And when the current slows down, the coil speeds it up. So, when the discharge of the capacitor is dying down, the coil makes the current keep going anyhow. This drains more electrons from the plate that used to have too many, and piles them up on the plate that had too few. Soon this plate has too many. The electrons are crowded on it, so they start streaming back the other way. The current keeps going back and forth in this way with a rapid rhythm.

Every oscillator has a natural rhythm that depends on the size of the capacitor and the coil. Radio stations regulate the rhythm or frequency at which they broadcast by using the proper coil and capacitor. Each station has a

122

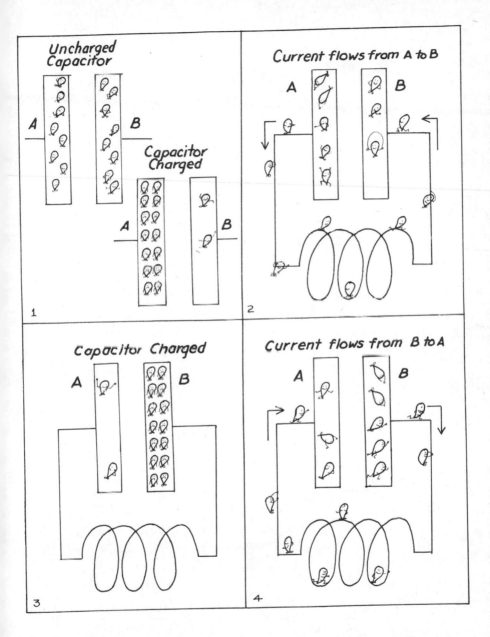

123

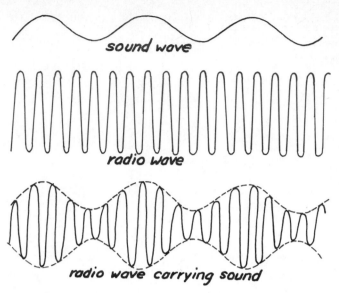

sound wave

radio wave

radio wave carrying sound

separate frequency assigned to it by the government. AM stations use frequencies from 550 thousand to 1,600 thousand cycles. FM and TV stations use frequencies from 57 million cycles to 213 million cycles.

In a radio broadcast, the sound vibrations of voices and music are turned into electrical vibrations. These are added to the radio waves, which then carry the sound with them out into space.

Plucking Music Out Of Space

Your radio receiver has a capacitor and coil team, too. This gives it a natural rhythm. When you turn the tuning dial, you change the size of the capacitor, and so you change the rhythm. Waves of many rhythms pass the antenna of your set. If the natural rhythm of your set matches one of them, the waves of that rhythm will make an electric current vibrate in your set, just as your singing can make a string in your piano vibrate. One part of your set picks up the radio message in this way. Another part separates the slower sound vibrations from the high-frequency vibrations, and then uses them to work the loud speaker.

Cutting Thin Slices Of Time

The slow decay of uranium gave us an atomic clock that can measure long intervals up to billions of years. The rapid vibrations in radio circuits give us an electronic clock that can measure tiny intervals down to billionths of a second.

One electronic clock is like the old-fashioned water clocks of Athens. Instead of a bowl of water, it uses a container of electrical power, the capacitor. The water flowed out of the bowl through a hole. The electricity flows out of the capacitor through a resistance. Just as the size of the hole controlled the time it took for the bowl to empty, the size of the resistance controls the time it takes for the capacitor to discharge. In this way, small slices of time are cut to order. This type of clock is often used in automatic machinery to control the turning on and off of switches.

Another kind of electronic clock is used to measure the time of very rapid events, like the flight of a bullet. This kind of clock has three main parts, an *oscillator*, a *gating circuit*, and a *counting circuit*. The oscillator makes high-frequency vibrations. The gating circuit opens the "gate" to admit the vibrations when the event begins. It closes the "gate" when the event ends. The counting circuit measures the time by counting how many vibrations passed through the "gate." If, for example, the vibrations have

125

a frequency of one million cycles, then each vibration takes one one-millionth of a second. If five vibrations pass through the "gate," it means that the time interval is five-millionths of a second.

The Language Clock

To learn about the newest of clocks, we now turn our backs on machines and gadgets, springs, pendulums, gears, atoms, and electricity, and we enter the quiet study of a language specialist. For the latest clock invented is a language clock. In 1950 American language specialists discovered that languages change at a steady rate through the centuries. So now they can use the amount of change in a language to measure time. This is how they have done it:

First they prepared a list of 200 things for which there are words in all languages. Then they compared these words in present-day and recent languages with the ancient languages from which they developed. They found that for some of the 200 things, the ancient words continued in use, though pronounced or written differently. But for others, new words had been adopted in the language. After a thousand years, on the average, 81 per cent of the words, or 162 of the 200 words, were unchanged. After two thousand years, 81 per cent of 81 per cent, or 66 percent, were unchanged. After three thousand years, 81 per cent of 66 per cent, or about 53 per cent, were unchanged, and so on.

If two languages have developed separately from the same ancient tongue, after a thousand years the mother language and each daughter language will have only 81 per cent of the 200 words in common. So the daughter

126

languages will have 81 per cent of 81 per cent, or 66 per cent in common. After two thousand years they will have 66 per cent of 66 per cent, or about 43 per cent, in common. After three thousand years they will have 66 per cent of 43 per cent, or about 29 per cent in common.

A long, long time ago some Eskimos left the mainland and settled in the Aleutian Islands off Alaska. Today the Aleutian language and the Eskimo language share only about 29 per cent of the words in the standard list of 200. This shows that the Aleutian Islands were settled about 3,000 years ago. Radio-carbon dating of the remains of early Aleutian settlements gives the same figure of 3,000 years.

On To The Future

Man has marched down the stream of time for about a million years. On his journey to civilization he learned that he lives in a world of many rhythms. He found rhythms high in the sky, and buried deep in the rocks. He found rhythms in the heart of the atom, and out in the far reaches of space. And, besides those that he found in nature, he learned how to make many more. By mastering these rhythms he developed the art of measuring time. So now he can measure time, not only for seconds, days, and years—not only for centuries—but for billions of years on the one hand, and a billionth of a second on the other. But his mastery of rhythm means more than the measurement of time. It means increasing control over nature. His knowledge of rhythms lights up the hidden, dark corners of the past. But it also helps him to plan the future. Armed with knowledge of the rhythms of the universe, man continues to march hopefully down the stream of time.

Appendix

Face north, and hold the star clock upside down over your head so that the N outside dial A is north of the center.

A Star Clock

To make the clock: Use stiff paper or thin cardboard. On one sheet trace dial A and the letters N, E and W near it. On another sheet, trace dial B with its pointer, and trace dial C. Cut out dial B (with the pointer which it contains), and cut out dial C. Make a pinhole at the center of each dial. Put dial B over dial A, and dial C over dial B, with their centers together. Hold them in place with a pin through their centers, or, even better, with a small bolt and nut or a snap fastener.

To use the clock: Follow the directions printed on dials A, B and C, in that order.

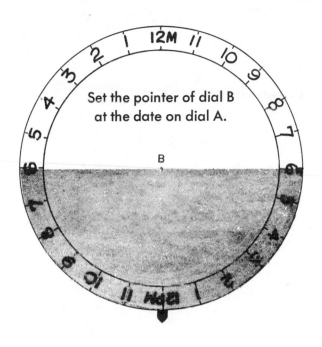

Set the pointer of dial B
at the date on dial A.

B

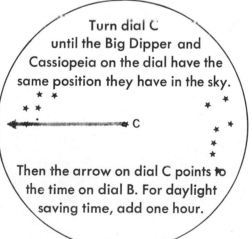

Turn dial C
until the Big Dipper and
Cassiopeia on the dial have the
same position they have in the sky.

C

Then the arrow on dial C points to
the time on dial B. For daylight
saving time, add one hour.

Index

130